empowered women with adhd

TOOLS, HACKS, AND PROVEN STRATEGIES TO MANAGE OVERWHELM, RACING THOUGHTS, AND EMOTIONS. THE COMPLETE GUIDE TO LIVING WITH CLARITY AND CONFIDENCE.

ESTELLE ROSE

ROSALI PUBLISHING

Illustrations (except cover) by Amber Anderson

First edition

contents

introduction

It was a scorching August day, the kind that makes your skin beg for a dip into the cool water. I had excitedly joined my friends for a much-anticipated beach picnic, daydreaming of laughter, delicious food, and the carefree atmosphere that only summer can bring. Little did I know that my own quirks, as a woman with ADHD, were about to turn this sunny day into an extraordinary tale.

As we spread our blankets and unpacked the goodies, panic washed over me like a wave. I had forgotten essential elements – plates, and cutlery. Now, you might assume I'd simply dash back home and retrieve them. If only my life could be that simple!

"Do we really need plates and cutlery?" I thought, looking at the tempting spread of salads I had painstakingly prepared. But amidst my musings, insecurities sprouted like wildflowers in the garden of my mind. What if I was the odd one out, the weirdo who couldn't navigate the simplest social expectations? I glanced at the group, their laughter and camaraderie reminded me of my perpetual feeling of not quite fitting in. Would anyone notice if I left for a few minutes? The fear of missing out, of being exposed as the eternal oddity, tugged at my heartstrings.

Summoning a surge of determination, I embarked on a seemingly straightforward walk home. However, my mind had a different plan in store for me, teasing my attention at every corner.

As I strolled along the sun-kissed path, my phone jolted with a familiar vibration. A harmless reminder to take my supplements, or so I thought. One innocent notification led to another, and before I knew it, I found myself spiraling down the rabbit hole of distraction. Curiosity teased my senses, pulling me deeper into the digital abyss.

Lost in a web of apps, my original mission became a distant memory. Emails demanded my attention as if they held the secrets to the universe. And speaking of secrets, my mind decided it was the perfect time to delve into the world of Rejection Sensitive Dysphoria (RSD). So, like an aimless wanderer in the realm of the internet, I indulged in an impromptu crash course on RSD.

It wasn't until I abruptly snapped back to reality that I realized I had neglected my friends for far too long. In a hasty attempt to make amends, I grabbed a frisbee and a shawl, my mind a whirlwind of conflicting priorities. Wait, what? A frisbee? I'm glad you're following because I didn't walk all the way back home to get a frisbee! But amidst all the distractions and the sudden rush to rejoin my companions, the plates and cutlery had evaporated from my thoughts.

Returning to the beach, I was met with a mix of concern and amusement from my friends. Apparently, my absence had stretched on for an hour, leaving them puzzled and slightly worried. I offered an apologetic smile, my hair still damp from a misadventure along the jetty at high tide—another result of my ADHD-induced wanderings. As water dripped from my soaked dress and the frisbee clung to my hand, I decided to embrace the humor of the situation.

Gathered around the crackling fire, we settled into a cozy circle, the flames casting a warm glow on our faces. And as I regaled my friends with tales of my unpredictable journey, laughter filled the air. Yet, beneath the lighthearted banter, I thought about all the struggles we face as women with ADHD.

And that's what this book is all about. But make no mistake, my friends, this isn't just a compilation of entertaining mishaps. This is a survival guide filled with tools and hacks that have helped me navigate the turbulent seas of ADHD and emerge stronger, wiser, and more determined than ever.

Fun and games aside, I understand your pain so well. In my experience, ADHD can feel like you're trying to juggle a million different things at once, and no matter how hard you try, you just can't keep all the balls in the air. The chaos in your life, the housework, organizing, especially when you have to manage the lives of those around you as well (like, you know, kids), can feel so overwhelming, and it's hard not to feel like you're drowning in a sea of responsibility.

I know these feelings all too well: the racing thoughts, the roller-coaster of emotions, the moods that change on a dime. All of this can leave you feeling like you're in a crazy video game and you lost the gamepad. It can be frustrating and exhausting to deal with, but it's okay to feel overwhelmed by it all.

But please know that you're not alone. So many of us, women with ADHD feel held back by our condition, like we're not living up to our full potential. You know you have moments of brilliance when you feel like you can conquer the world. I mean, do you remember how efficient you were the last time you hyperfocused on a project? But sadly, these moments can be overshadowed by the times when you feel completely useless. It's a tough balance to strike, but you don't have to figure it out by yourself.

Just remember that ADHD doesn't have to hold you back. You are so much more than your diagnosis, and with the right tools and support, you can learn to manage the overwhelm, calm your mind, make peace with your brain, and achieve your goals in both work and relationships.

Let me give it to you straight: I'm not selling you a magic pill. This change won't happen overnight, but you are capable of so much more than you realize.

I want you to know that there is hope and that this book is your guide on your journey toward managing your ADHD and living a more fulfilling life. Within these pages, you'll find practical strategies and clear, actionable steps to help you manage overwhelming thoughts and emotions. You'll learn how to navigate relationships with friends, family, and professionals and effectively communicate your needs.

This book is based on the latest evidence-based research and information on ADHD, specifically tailored to the unique experiences of women. We'll talk about societal stigmas and hormones too. It's important to understand ourselves better, and we'll explore the ways in which ADHD affects you and your life. But we won't stop there - we'll also look at how to leverage your ADHD strengths and empower you just as you are.

These pages will help you live with clarity and confidence, despite the challenges of ADHD. You'll find practical strategies to help you keep your racing thoughts in check, your space organized, and your confidence high. We will even tackle the floordrobe (you know, that pile of clothes on the floor). Sure, you might still forget your keys occasionally, but it won't be nearly as overwhelming anymore!

We'll also explore ways to improve your self-esteem and cultivate self-love and self-compassion, the true form of self-care. Ultimately, you'll learn to make peace with your brain and give yourself the love you deserve.

After reading what I have in store for you, you'll feel a sense of relief and empowerment that you may not have felt before. You'll have a newfound understanding of your ADHD, how it affects you, and the practical strategies for managing it. You'll be better equipped to communicate your needs and advocate for yourself. You'll feel more confident in your ability to navigate the challenges of ADHD, and you'll be able to see the strengths and potential that lie within you.

But hey, hold on a second! You might wonder, "How would you know what I need?" Well, let me tell you something—I'm here as someone who's been in your shoes.

You see, I'm a messy creative mother of two with a late ADHD diagnosis. I've experienced the challenges and triumphs firsthand. Like many with ADHD, I've had more career changes than cats have lives! Most of them in the creative industries. The pattern is familiar: the excitement, the intense learning, the career pursuit, and the anticipation of the next challenge.

It was seven years ago when a friend visited me during a search for my next dream career. That day, she declared that I should become a coach because I was so good at empowering others. And so, I did. I began coaching young women embarking on their creative careers, guiding them through mindset, self-esteem, goals, produc-tivity, accountability, and social skills. Along the way, I shared the transformative tools I had gathered over the years to navigate the freelance world with ADHD, and I picked up new ones.

But more importantly, I've dedicated the past 27 years, if not my entire life, to experimenting on myself. I've pursued endless research, devoured books, and completed trainings and therapies. I picked up countless strategies to manage ADHD symptoms, even before I fully understood them as such. And now, I'm eager to share that wealth of knowledge with you.

Besides that, I was born in Paris and lived in the UK for 16 years and by the sea for 13 years. What else? Oh yeah, I'm more of a cat person than a dog person, and I hate cucumbers. Wait... am I over-sharing? Let's not go on a tangent about cats and cucumbers.

Anyways, you might be thinking to yourself, "Well, that's all well and good, but how will any of this help *me*?". Well, hear me out, friend: despite being a high-achiever (hello masking), I used to feel frazzled all the time and constantly switch from feeling either full of beans to completely fatigued. I also felt held back, like I should be so much further and achieve so much more.

Now, I have not just made peace with my messy and scattered tendencies, I have also learned to temper the impairing symptoms and embrace my wonderful ADHD brain. Speaking of the wonders of ADHD brains, when I hyperfocus on a subject, I want to learn everything there is to know about it - and, of course, that includes ADHD!

Helping you live your life to your full potential matters deeply to me because I have firsthand experience with how challenging it can be to manage ADHD. I know the struggles and victories of living with this condition. But I also know it's possible to thrive with ADHD rather than just survive. That's why I'm passionate about sharing the hacks that can help you make ADHD work with you rather than against you.

Simply put, I'm writing the book I wish was around when I discovered I might have ADHD. I wish I had read this book when I first looked for ways to manage ADHD besides medication. And "Empowered women empower women." I believe that by sharing my personal experiences and strategies, I can help other women with ADHD find peace and live happy, fulfilling lives.

This book is my way of telling you that, yes, sometimes you'll find yourself bringing back a frisbee instead of plates, but it doesn't have to hold you back from having the best picnic of your life! With the gold mine of knowledge I've penned down within these pages, you'll learn how to turn your ADHD quirks into skills that will help you throughout your life.

And you know what? I can't wait to see the amazing things you'll achieve.

So let's dive in and get started on this journey together. Remember, you're not alone in this - I'm here to support you every step of the way. Let's make ADHD work with us, not against us!

BEFORE YOU START

Get your
Empowered ADHD Planners Pack,
the perfect companion to this book,
to start taking control of your time,
racing thoughts and emotions
immediately.

Free planners   A GIFT FOR YOU   Download now

DOWNLOAD NOW

Follow this link:
bit.ly /
EmpoweredPlanners

or scan the
QR code

how to use this book

Let me just give you a few pointers before diving into the juicy bits.

First things first: let's address the elephant in the room. This book does not substitute a professional diagnosis, treatment, or therapy. I'm not a psychiatrist, just a fellow ADHDer sharing my experiences and strategies that have helped me along the way. So please do NOT hesitate to ever reach out to a medical professional for help.

TAKE WHAT you WANT...
& LEAVE the REST

You might find that you deeply resonate with some of these pages. So grab the lessons you find invaluable, cherish them, and use them. But there might be some symptoms that you will find less relevant to your situation, so feel free to skip those parts. You don't have to try every single strategy offered in this book.

Some strategies are more practical than others, depending on what else is happening in your life. Managing ADHD symptoms is trickier if you're a single mom managing four kids and two jobs. But I'm confident you will find tools you need regardless. So when I say, "Find what works for you," I also mean, "Find what works for you in your current situation."

I've written the book with the idea that it will be read in full, so later chapters refer to earlier ones. I recommend reading the book in order but going faster on the parts that are less relevant to you and staying longer on the ones that really hit home.

COME BACK

You know those parts you found really useful? Come back to them, revisit them later, check in with yourself. And circumstances often change, so strategies that were not relevant to you before might become relevant a few months from now. So keep coming back.

Keeping a journal alongside this book can be a great idea. You can jot down tips and tools that you learn and keep track of what works best for you. It's important to give some time for strategies to work, so keep going if something doesn't work right away.

And remember, everyone's journey with ADHD is unique, so what works for someone else may not work for you and vice versa. Take things one step at a time, and start with one strategy before moving on to the next. Small changes can lead to big improvements over time!

Just by reading this book and learning about ADHD, you're already taking a huge step toward better understanding yourself. So, don't feel pressured to try every tip and tool in the book. Simply understanding how ADHD affects you as a woman can be incredibly empowering and help you find the right path forward for yourself.

Self-compassion is key, and seeking the right help is always a good idea.

Now, you will see that I sometimes mention apps, books, or products. But let me put it out there, I have no vested interest in recommending those, okay? I have no shares or referral scheme with them. It's just me sharing some apps and other tools that I have tried and found useful. Plus, most of the apps are free.

So please take what you need, try it out, and don't be afraid to explore things on your own. Remember, an ADHD diagnosis is not the end. In fact, it's just the beginning, so let's get started on our journey together.

CHAPTER ONE

empowered women and adhd

UNDERSTAND ADHD, UNDERSTAND YOURSELF

ADHD, also known as Attention Deficit Hyperactivity Disorder, is a neurological condition affecting both children and adults. Think of it as having a noisy brain that can't sit still, like a super excited puppy that just wants to jump and run around all the time (and sometimes chase its own tail).

To put it simply, people with ADHD can struggle with things like paying attention, staying organized, and controlling impulses. We're often mega-forgetful, easily distracted, and have trouble completing tasks.

But you haven't picked up this book to hear that! We both know your ADHD symptoms are a lot more complicated than that. Heck, we both know your life is a lot more complicated than that! But don't fret. We are going to take a closer look at ADHD. Why? Because understanding ADHD is the first step to managing it.

1. WHAT IS ADHD?

Before we dive into the complexity of the symptoms, let's start with the basics, shall we?

THE BASICS

The usual cause given for ADHD is an imbalance of two key neurotransmitters in the brain: norepinephrine and dopamine.

Norepinephrine

Norepinephrine is a hormone that helps regulate attention, alertness, mood, memory, and our sleep-wake cycle. You might have heard about it under its other name, noradrenaline. I'm sure you can already see how its functions relate to ADHD symptoms, as our ADHD brains may not produce enough of this hormone.

PEOPLE with ADHD can be MEGA FORGETFUL, EASILY DISTRACTED + have TROUBLE COMPLETING TASKS...

Dopamine

Dopamine, on the other hand, is a chemical that helps nerve cells communicate with each other. On top of memory and mood, it also regulates motivation, movement, and addiction. You see, dopamine is big in our reward system. It gets released when we do something enjoyable, like eating chocolate or getting likes on social media, which then motivates us to seek that reward again.

In people with ADHD, the brain may not produce enough dopamine, and you can immediately see the association with classic ADHD symptoms, right?

In a nutshell, ADHD is caused by an imbalance of norepinephrine and dopamine in the brain. I'm telling you all this because understanding the underlying biology of ADHD can help us develop effective strategies for managing its symptoms.

FACTS VS. FICTION

Oh, boy, there are plenty of misconceptions out there when it comes to ADHD! Let's dive in and separate fact from fiction.

> Fiction: ADHD is just an excuse for bad behavior.

> Fact: Nope, sorry, that's just not true. ADHD is a real neurological condition that affects how the brain processes information and regulates attention and behavior.

> Fiction: ADHD only affects hyperactive children.

> Fact: While hyperactivity is one of the hallmark symptoms of ADHD, it can also manifest as inattention or impulsivity. And guess what? ADHD doesn't magically disappear once you hit adulthood.

3

Fiction: ADHD only affects boys.

Fact: If only! For a long time, ADHD was seen as a boy's condition. At best, it was considered a boys and men issue. But we now know that ADHD affects girls and women too, which is what we're about to dive deeply into.

Fiction: ADHD is caused by bad parenting or too much screen time.

Fact: Sorry, Charlie, but that's just not the case. While environmental factors like parenting and screen time can certainly influence a child's behavior, they don't cause ADHD. ADHD is a complex condition with a genetic component, meaning it's likely inherited from one or both parents.

Fiction: People with ADHD can't focus on anything.

Fact: While difficulty with focus and attention is a key symptom of ADHD, it's not quite as black-and-white as "can't focus on anything." People with ADHD may struggle to sustain attention on uninteresting tasks. Still, they can often hyperfocus on tasks they find stimulating or enjoyable.

Fiction: Medication is the only treatment for ADHD.

Fact: While medication can be an effective tool for managing ADHD symptoms, it's by no means the only option and often not enough on its own. In fact, most psychiatrists will recommend lifestyle changes too. And you're in luck because this is what this book is about - non-medical strategies to manage your ADHD.

Fiction: Everyone has ADHD symptoms, like forgetting things or procrastinating.

Fact: To a degree, yes. But not to the same degree, and it can be very unhelpful, even hurtful, to hear this while trying to get a diagnosis. As we'll soon see, there is a lot more to having ADHD than forgetting our car keys.

Well, there you have it. The next time someone tries to lecture you about your condition, you'll have a few comebacks up your sleeve.

THE CAUSES

Let's talk about the causes of ADHD - and no, it's not because you drank too much soda as a kid!

The truth is, ADHD is a complex condition with many factors at play. Some possible causes include genetics, brain chemistry, and environmental factors like prenatal exposure to toxins.

But honestly, it's like trying to untangle a knot of spaghetti. There's no one simple cause, and it's likely a combination of different factors unique to each individual.

The controversy

While we have some ideas about the possible causes of ADHD, it's important to note that the exact origins of the condition are still being debated in the scientific community.

Some experts believe it's primarily caused by genetic factors, while others suggest that environmental factors like diet or early childhood trauma could play a role.

To complicate things even further, the symptoms of ADHD can sometimes be mistaken for other conditions, which muddies the waters when it comes to diagnosis and treatment.

Hereditary or nah?

Picture this: you're sitting down to dinner with your family, and suddenly your aunt announces that she's always had trouble with focus and organization - just like you! Is it possible that ADHD is inherited?

The short answer is yes - there is strong evidence to suggest that genetics can play a crucial role in the development of ADHD. But here's where things get a little complicated: it's not 100% for sure, and not all cases of ADHD are inherited.

In fact, a study published in the journal *Lancet* suggests that only about half of all ADHD cases are linked to genetic factors. The other half may be caused by environmental factors. The researchers explain that "ADHD is highly heritable and multifactorial; multiple genes and non-inherited factors contribute to the disorder."

So it's not a clear-cut case of nature vs. nurture - it's a bit of both and probably a unique mix for each of us!

THE MORBID COMORBIDITIES

Did you know that up to 70% of people with ADHD have at least one comorbid condition? That's right, ADHD loves to hang out with other conditions like anxiety, depression, and learning disorders. They're a package deal!

If you're living with ADHD, chances are you're no stranger to the concept of comorbidity - that is, the idea that ADHD often coexists alongside other conditions. It's like having a sidekick, but instead of Batman and Robin, it's ADHD and [insert other condition here].

Some of the most common sidekicks (err, comorbidities) of ADHD include learning disorders (dyslexia, dyscalculia, etc.), anxiety, depression, sensory processing disorder, and oppositional defiant disorder. It's like playing a giant game of Tetris in our heads, and the pieces don't even fit.

But here's the thing: while dealing with more than one condition at a time can be frustrating, recognizing comorbidity is actually a good thing. Why? Same reason you might want an ADHD diagnosis! It means you can target it and look for effective treatments that address all of your symptoms, not just some of them.

So while ADHD may be the star of the show, don't forget about its trusty sidekicks - they may be causing some trouble. Still, with the right strategies and help, you can all learn to work together in perfect harmony (or at least a little bit more peacefully).

THE SUBTYPES

So ADHD people come in all shapes and sizes, and as we know, we're all different. There are many reasons why my ADHD symptoms look very different from my 10-year-old nephew's ADHD symptoms. One of them could be that our ADHD type might be different. Enter ADHD subtypes! Each with its own unique set of quirks and challenges.

Inattentive type

Sometimes called the "daydreamer" type. If you have the inattentive type of ADHD, you might struggle with paying attention to details, following through on tasks, and staying organized. But on the bright side, you might have a vivid imagination and a knack for thinking outside the box.

Hyperactive-impulsive type

If you have hyperactive-impulsive type ADHD, you're always on the go and might find sitting still to be quite difficult. You're likely to be constantly fidgeting and squirming. You might also blurt out your thoughts without thinking first, which can get you into trouble. But hey, at least you have a lot of energy and probably a high metabolism, right?

Combined type

As the name suggests, this type of ADHD combines the other two types. If you have combined type ADHD, you might struggle with both inattention and hyperactivity/impulsivity. So, good luck, my friend! No, just kidding. Like all types, it is about knowing yourself and developing the strategies that work for you.

Just like how we all have our unique fingerprints, we all have our own unique ADHD experiences. We have different symptoms, different strengths, and different struggles. What works for one person might not work for another. It's like a choose-your-own-adventure book, except it's your own ADHD journey. So don't get too caught up in comparing yourself to others or feeling like you're not doing ADHD "right." There is no right or wrong way to have ADHD - it's all about finding what works for you.

2. WOMEN AND ADHD

So let's ask the question we've all been waiting for - what does it mean to be a woman when it comes to ADHD? Why is it that women get diagnosed later in life? And what is the deal with those pesky hormones? Well, we're about to jump headfirst into it all!

WOMEN OR WOMXN

Well, first of all, let's get one thing straight: when I say "woman" and "women," I'm talking about anyone who identifies as a woman, regardless of what gender they were assigned at birth. That means transwomen, gender nonconforming people, and anyone else who feels they belong here. You're welcome here because we know that ADHD doesn't discriminate based on gender identity.

Actually, a review study on "Increased Gender Variance in Autism Spectrum Disorders and Attention Deficit Hyperactivity Disorder" published in 2014, states that "evidence suggests over-representation of autism spectrum disorders (ASDs) and behavioral difficulties among people referred for gender issues". Basically, individuals who are transgender or gender nonconforming (TGNC) may experience ADHD at higher rates than cisgender individuals. TGNC individuals may face additional challenges and stress that can exacerbate ADHD symptoms, such as discrimination, isolation, and a lack of access to supportive healthcare services.

And there is even more evidence. A study published in the *Journal of Autism and Developmental Disorders* found that transgender and nonbinary youth were more likely to show symptoms of ADHD than cisgender youth. Another study published in the *Journal of Consulting and Clinical Psychology* found that transgender adults were significantly more likely to report symptoms of inattention, hyperactivity, and impulsivity compared to cisgender adults.

The reasons for this imbalance are complex and not yet fully understood but may include a combination of genetic and environmental factors. Hormonal treatments, such as hormone replacement therapy, can also affect brain chemistry and potentially impact ADHD symptoms.

Overall, more research is needed to fully understand the relationship between ADHD and gender identity. Still, it's clear that TGNC individuals may face unique challenges when managing ADHD symptoms.

Oh and hey there, cis-men! Don't let the title of this book scare you off. While it's written with women with ADHD in mind, that doesn't mean you're not allowed here. If you've been struggling with overwhelm, having racing thoughts, and feeling held back by ADHD, and you think you can benefit from the strategies here, then you're in the right place. And if you want to read this book to support the ADHD women in your life, you're very welcome to stay too.

WHY ARE WOMEN DIAGNOSED LATER?

Well, the world of ADHD diagnosis is a bit like a treasure hunt, and unfortunately for women, the treasure chest is usually buried pretty deep. It's not that women are bad at finding treasure; it's just that the map was drawn for someone else.

Historically, ADHD has been considered a boy's disorder, so when women present symptoms that don't fit the typical mold, doctors can be quick to dismiss the possibility of ADHD. But thankfully, the map is starting to get updated. ADHD is increasingly recognized in women, and the diagnosis rate is slowly catching up.

Lack of research

So because ADHD was considered a disorder that mostly affected males, much of the research was focused on them. As a result, the symptoms of ADHD in women were often overlooked or misdiagnosed as something else.

Fortunately, more research is now being done to better understand how ADHD affects women, leading to more accurate diagnoses and better treatment options. So, if you're a woman who suspects you might have ADHD, don't give up hope and talk to your doctor. There's a growing understanding and recognition of how ADHD presents in women, and with the right support, you can thrive.

Social norms

Ever heard of the "good girl" narrative? The idea is that girls should be quiet, organized, and obedient. It's a societal construct that's been drilled into our heads from a young age. It's no wonder that girls with ADHD often go undiagnosed until later in life. After all, if you're not causing trouble and doing well or well enough in school, who will think to look for something like ADHD?

But as we grow older and take on more responsibilities, the demands on our functional abilities increase. Work, family, and relationships all require us to be organized and focused. And for women, that's often when ADHD symptoms start to become more noticeable. That was certainly the case for me.

It's important to remember that the "good girl" narrative is just that - a narrative. It's not based on fact or science. And it certainly doesn't mean that girls can't have ADHD.

HORMONES

Alright, let's talk hormones! They can affect so many things in our bodies and minds - our mood, skin, and energy levels... so it's no surprise they will also affect our ADHD symptoms!

For those of us who menstruate, our ADHD symptoms can get worse during certain times of the month (hello PMS!), and for those of us going through menopause, it can be a whole new ball game.

But here's the thing - despite the fact that hormones can have a big impact on our ADHD, it's not always taken into consideration when it comes to medication or treatment in general. It's like our hormones are just an afterthought - "Oh yeah, those might have an effect, I guess." We need more studies and research to really understand how hormones impact our ADHD and how we can manage it better.

But don't worry; we will take a much deeper dive into how hormones can affect ADHD and what we can do about it when we reach Chapter 5.

ADHD SYMPTOMS FOR WOMEN

A research review published in the *Journal of Abnormal Child Psychology* in 2021 investigated gender differences in ADHD symptoms and impairment in a large community sample. It was found that "Females are more likely to present inattention symptoms and associated internalizing problems".

So women with ADHD are more likely to present with the predominantly inattentive type, which means that they may have trouble with focus, organization, time management, and forgetfulness. We also tend to experience more internal symptoms. It can look like daydreaming or being easily distracted (you know, by shiny objects or squirrels).

Additionally, women may develop coping mechanisms, such as perfectionism and people-pleasing, that can mask their ADHD symptoms. This is important to keep in mind because it's another reason for late diagnoses. It can make it more difficult for healthcare professionals to spot and lead to women being misdiagnosed with anxiety or depression instead of ADHD.

Here are just a few examples of ADHD symptoms that women might experience:

- Forgetting important appointments, meetings, and deadlines like it's your full-time job.
- Feeling like you're constantly running late, no matter how hard you try to be on time.
- Constantly losing your keys, phone, wallet, and other important items.
- Starting a task with all the enthusiasm in the world, only to abandon it halfway through and move on to something else.
- Procrastinating until the very last minute, then working like a mad woman to meet the deadline.
- Being easily distracted by your environment (back to that squirrel).
- Struggling to follow conversations, especially in noisy or crowded settings.
- Feeling overwhelmed by even small tasks, like making a grocery list or doing the dishes.
- Struggling to stay organized, both in your physical space and thoughts.
- Talking a mile a minute and interrupting others without realizing it.
- Feeling like you're always in your head and can't shut off your thoughts.

And that's just scratching the surface. If any of these sound familiar, you might want to stick around! And no, you don't have to tick all the boxes to be part of the club.

CHAPTER TWO

empowered mindset

SHIFT YOUR MINDSET, EMBRACE NEURODIVERSITY, AND LEARN TO LOVE ADHD

WELCOME to the chapter that proves you're absolutely fabulous, darling! Yes, you read that right. Despite what society may have told you, having ADHD does not mean you're broken. In fact, we have many reasons to love ADHD. I'll give you 15 reasons in a bit, but honestly, there are far more.

This chapter also gives you the sociological background to ADHD, so by the end, you'll feel like you have a deeper understanding of yourself and your place in the world. So get ready to feel empowered and excited to take action because the following chapters become more and more practical. But it won't do any good without adopting the right mindset. So let's start with that.

1. 5 STRATEGIES TO SHIFT YOUR MINDSET

"Mindset" is a word that gets thrown around a lot. It's a bit of a buzzword, and if it makes you cringe, please just bear with me for a second. Simply put, your mindset is how you see yourself and the world around you. It is the values and belief systems that are ingrained in your mind. And guess what? These have an impact on how you think, feel, and behave.

So having a positive mindset can make a huge difference in how you approach challenges and setbacks not only in your life but with your ADHD symptoms as well.

With a positive mindset, you're more likely to reframe your thoughts to focus on growth and progress instead of getting stuck in negative self-talk. So put on your positivity cape and prepare to look at the mindsets that will help you work *with* your ADHD.

I'm aware that all this mindset talk can sound very *woo-woo*, but there is actual proof! Many studies have demonstrated the impact of mindset on resilience, including a recent one by Michael Wolcott, published in *Medical Education*, looking at the role of mindset in the healing process in healthcare. He states that growth mindset is "a way to fine-tune our engines and enhance our miles per gallon (or kilometres per litre depending on your location) that prevents us from depleting our tanks."

Actually, it gets even better - our brains are like Play-Doh that never hardens! We can mold it and shape it into whatever we want. And, yes, even if we have ADHD.

In a more *sciencey* way, neuroplasticity is the brain's ability to change and adapt over time. It was once thought that the brain stopped developing after childhood, but a major study conducted by a team at Harvard Medical School in the early 2000s has shown that it is actually malleable even as an adult.

So that means that we can rewire our brains at any time, thanks to neuroplasticity! Aren't you excited that we can develop new neural pathways and change how we think and behave, no matter how old we are? I am!

This is especially important for us with ADHD because it means we can still make changes and improve our lives despite being diagnosed late and having years of struggles. It is not a fatality, our brains are not set in stone, and while we can't cure ADHD, we have the ability to make changes and improve our functioning and live a better life.

Sold yet? Interested in developing a growth mindset? Great! Let's have a look at five simple strategies:

1. Your past does not predict your future

Being late to the ADHD party isn't a big deal! Although we may have missed out on some important information that could have helped in childhood, we've probably developed coping mechanisms that have helped us get this far. So instead of dwelling on the past, let's celebrate that we can now focus on creating a brighter and kinder future for ourselves. It's never too late. Seriously, I've met a woman who was diagnosed at 72, so if you can beat that, please get in touch.

Now, join me in giving ourselves a big hug and recognizing that our past doesn't define us. We're not broken, and now that we know what it's called, we can start to address ADHD and explore new tools and strategies to thrive.

2. Compare yourself to yourself

It's easy to look at someone's social media feed and think, "Wow, they have it all together! Their life is perfect!" But let me tell you a little secret - no one's got it all figured out. And I'm sure you know that social media posts are highly curated and often don't accurately reflect someone's real life. I'll tell you an even bigger secret: writing a book about it doesn't mean you have it all together either. But don't tell anyone, okay?

The truth is, we all have our own individual struggles that are often invisible to the people around us. And that's okay! Comparing each other's symptoms for validation and inspiration is great, but we also need to focus on our own journey and growth. Measure progress according to your own timeline, not your peers' results.

3. See the humor in ADHD

Having ADHD can sometimes feel like a yo-yo, except you're the yo-yo and not the hand that controls it. One moment you're hyperfocused and getting things done at the speed of light; the next, you're easily distracted and struggling to stay on task. But let's not beat ourselves up over it; let's adopt the philosophy of "oh well."

In the past, when I forgot to bring something, like cutlery to a picnic, I used to get super frustrated with myself and say things like, "What an idiot," or "I'm so stupid!" I'm now trying to see the humor in it. I try to think, "Oh well, my brain was busy with something else," and that's okay!

So, embrace your quirks and use "oh well" to laugh at the ups and downs of having ADHD. And remember, you're not alone in this journey.

4. Experimental mindset

Let's say you're trying to make cookies. Even if you have found the perfect recipe, your oven is unique, and you will have to experiment with cooking time and temperature.

Did someone say cookies? Mmm… Cookies…

Okay, back to the experimental mindset!

So it's the same as a new recipe; adopting an experimental mindset means trying out different approaches and strategies to life problems and finding what works best for your unique oven. Erm, sorry, I mean life!

So time to swap the superhero cape for a lab coat and goggles and pretend you are the lead scientist in the experiment of life. You can try new techniques, evaluate their effectiveness, and tweak them until they work for you.

5. Curious accountability

You can keep your goggles on because curious accountability goes hand in hand with an experimental mindset. But this time, when things don't go as planned, approach it with curiosity instead of beating yourself up. Ask yourself, "What can I learn from this?"

Curious accountability means being curious about why something worked or didn't work without blaming yourself. It means being accountable for your actions and choices while being open to learning and growing.

When you approach your ADHD management with a curious accountability mindset, you are more likely to find strategies that work for you and less likely to get discouraged by setbacks or failures.

So keep those in mind, and above all else, remember that you are not broken. There is always room for growth and improvement.

2. EMBRACING NEURODIVERSITY

So, here's the deal: society has this weird obsession with "normal." You know, being just like everyone else, following the same rules, fitting in, blah blah blah. But "normal" is overrated. Neurodiversity is the natural variation in how our brains work.

THE SOCIAL MODEL OF DISABILITY

The social model of disability was a huge eye-opener for me. Basically, it is a model that says that disability is not just an individual trait or medical condition but rather a social construct created by societal barriers and attitudes that prevent people with impairments from fully participating in society. And you know what? That applies to ADHD, too.

So for us, the impairment might be difficulty focusing, organizing thoughts, or remembering things. But the disability comes from the societal barriers that make it harder for us to succeed, like rigid work structures or a lack of understanding and empathy from others.

For example, a workplace requiring you to sit for long periods and focus on repetitive tasks can be challenging for someone with ADHD. However, if that workplace were to implement more flexible working arrangements, such as allowing for more frequent breaks or the ability to work on different tasks throughout the day, it could make a big difference and allow someone with ADHD to thrive.

Embracing neurodiversity and the social model of disability means recognizing that differences in how our brains work should not be seen as deficits but rather as valuable and valid differences that contribute to the richness and diversity of the human experience. By focusing on removing the barriers that disable us, rather than trying to "fix" ourselves, we can create a more inclusive and accepting society for all. Doesn't it sound nice?

This book isn't about helping you fit into a predetermined mold or becoming another cog in the machine. No, it's about embracing your unique quirks and differences and carving out your own path. It's about showing yourself some compassion and allowing yourself to be yourself - ADHD and all. It's about working hand in hand with ADHD rather than pretending it's not there.

No, I'm not talking about the carnival or wearing your superhero mask (although that could be fun, too). In the context of ADHD, masking is when someone consciously or unconsciously suppresses their ADHD symptoms to better fit into society's expectations. I was absolutely 100% guilty of this until fairly recently.

Masking can lead to stress and anxiety, as people with ADHD try to keep up appearances and hide their struggles. But you know what's better than masking? Unmasking! It's like taking off a tight pair of shoes after a long day. Aahhh...

Unmasking is when someone embraces their true self and lets their ADHD traits shine through. It's like saying, "I'm not scared to be seen - I make no apologies, this is me - Oh-oh-oh-oh" And if a drunken karaoke interpretation of *The Greatest Showman* is not your jam, I'm sure you'll find another creative way of expressing yourself.

But wait, "Is masking all bad?" I hear you cry. "Are you telling me to unmask right here, right now, Estelle? But how? That's the way I've known for years. I'm scared." I hear you. That's completely understandable, but let's all take a deep breath, rewind a bit, and explore the pros and cons.

Pros of masking:

- It can make it easier to fit in with neurotypical peers.
- It can help prevent social isolation and bullying.
- It can make it easier to navigate certain environments, such as school or work.
- It can help us feel more in control of our symptoms.

Cons of masking:

- It can be exhausting and stressful to maintain over time.
- It can lead to feelings of disconnection or inauthenticity.
- It can prevent us from seeking the support or accommodations we need.

- It can lead to burnout or other mental health challenges, such as anxiety or depression.

So, no, you don't have to take your whole mask off right here, right now. It's usually a slow process and something we gradually feel more comfortable with as time passes. It's just something to be aware of. Like everything else, this is your own journey, and you will find the right balance between masking and unmasking. By shifting our mindset and embracing neurodiversity, the mask will start to slide off organically.

3. 15 Things To Love About ADHD

While living with ADHD can have its challenges, there are also many things to love about having an ADHD brain. Yes, you heard that right! ADHD is not just a disorder. From hyper-focusing on things that interest you to having a never-ending supply of creativity, ADHD can give you an edge in so many ways. Recognizing those positive sides of ADHD will help shift your mindset and, ultimately, how you see ADHD and yourself.

1. Hyperfocus

You know that feeling when you're so deep into something that time seems to disappear? That's the magic of ADHD hyperfocus! When we're interested in something, we become completely absorbed in the task and everything around us disappears. We might lose track of time, forget to eat, drink, or even sleep.

But here's the thing - this intense focus can lead to amazing productivity! When you're in the hyperfocus zone, you have a concentration superpower that can help you accomplish incredible things in record time.

And it's not just quantity, it's quality too! The level of dedication and passion that comes with hyperfocus can lead to some awe-inspiring results. The trick is to use it as a powerful tool, whether working on a project or pursuing a hobby, and balance it with rest.

But more about that later, mainly in Chapter 7, when we'll talk about work.

2. Resilience

This is such an important life skill! And we are like superheroes when it comes to bouncing back from setbacks. You know that feeling when you fall off your bike and scrape your knee? Well, we might fall off our bikes and scrape our knees, but then we get back up and ride even faster than before. ADHD can make life challenging, but it also gives us a unique ability to bounce back.

And the best part is, we don't just bounce back from failures - with curious accountability on our side, we learn from them too.

So keep on bouncing, little Joey, and keep on being awesome!

3. People Person

Any social butterfly reading this book? I thought so. Individuals with ADHD tend to have a way with people that others can envy. We have an innate ability to connect and build meaningful relationships with our unfiltered thoughts and lively personality.

Sure, comorbidities such as anxieties can get in the way, but broadly speaking, our hyperactive and impulsive nature can make us the life of the party.

Even better, we tend to be sensitive to others' emotions, which makes us great at understanding people and building relationships based on mutual understanding and support.

4. Conversationalist

You see, we tend to have a lot of thoughts swirling around in our heads at any given moment. This means that when we start talking, it can be like opening the floodgates of a dam. Suddenly, all of those thoughts and ideas come pouring out, often in a rapid-fire, stream-of-consciousness kind of way.

Okay, this conversational style can be a bit overwhelming for some people. Still, if we tame it a little for those who want to stick around, that can make for some seriously entertaining conversations. And who doesn't like stand-up comedy?

We also have a unique perspective on things and are not afraid to share it. Some find it refreshing, and I like to call it candid! We're also great at connecting seemingly unrelated topics, which can lead to fascinating discussions.

5. Generosity and Empathy

While some may see ADHD as a deficit, I see it as an asset when it comes to connecting with others. We don't simply talk at people - our tendency to be highly attuned to the emotions of those around us makes us excellent empathizers. We often pick up on other people's feelings and needs without even trying, sometimes even a bit too much.

But it's not just empathy that we're great at - generosity is also a hallmark of ADHD. When we're interested in something or someone, we tend to throw our whole selves into it. That can mean giving generously of our time, resources, and energy. We sure know how to make a difference in the lives of those around us!

6. Compassion and Kindness

Because we often feel like outsiders ourselves, we know what it's like to feel misunderstood and marginalized. This gives us a unique perspective and makes us more willing to extend kindness and compassion to others.

We might overshare, but we are great listeners too. Paired with the innate ability to see past the surface level and get to the heart of a matter, we can be very supportive friends. Our openness and warmth can make people feel comfortable and understood in an exceptional way.

7. A Strong Sense of Justice

Our compassion and empathy also give us a powerful sense of what's fair and what's not, and we're not afraid to speak up when we see an injustice. Another trait where our superhero nature shines through!

As we can be very persuasive talkers and understand what it's like to feel different and excluded, we can be great advocates for marginalized or oppressed people. We're not afraid to stand up for ourselves or others, even if it means going against the status quo.

In fact, you will find many people with ADHD in activism for social justice causes. We can use our energy and enthusiasm to make a real difference in the world.

8. Risk-taking abilities

Have you ever found yourself in a situation where everyone is too scared to take a risk? Maybe they're too afraid of failure or too worried about what other people might think. Well, that's where those of us with ADHD come in!

Thanks to our limited filters and our ability to speak up and make unique connections, we have a special ability to take risks, which can lead to some pretty amazing things.

Just to be clear, I'm not talking about jumping from roof to roof here. You look after yourself, okay? And yes, risk-taking can get us into trouble, but it can also create unique experiences and opportunities.

It takes a lot of courage to take risks, so own it, woman - it's something to be proud of.

9. Determination

Okay, so we might often give up because we get bored once a task stops being interesting, or if it is so challenging, we don't know where to start.

But on the other hand, we have a strong sense of determination when it comes to something we're passionate about and are able to see the big picture and long-term goals. Pair it with hyperfocus, risk-taking, or even social justice, and boom - we're unstoppable.

Take American gymnast Simone Biles. Did you know she has ADHD? Can you just imagine how much determination it takes to become one of the most decorated gymnasts in history? Wow, am I right? [Cue applause]

10. Spontaneous Spirit

I guess that's the positive name for our impulsivity. And yes, it's not ideal when it comes to compulsive purchases we can't afford. Still, it is also the spark that ignites new ideas and can make even the dullest tasks seem like a thrilling challenge.

While it might scare some people off, it can definitely make us exciting to be around and just a general joy to follow on adventures.

Paired with an experimental mindset, we can see that sometimes the best things in life are the ones we never saw coming.

11. The funny bone

How many people with ADHD does it take to change a light bulb? Let's go ride bikes!

Funny? Yeah, maybe not, but people with ADHD are known for their unique sense of humor and infectious laughter.

Our brains are wired to make connections between seemingly unrelated things, leading to some pretty hilarious observations and jokes. Our tendency to see the absurdities in situations that others might overlook, paired with our gift of gab, can really help us make light of the problem.

But it's not just about being the class clown. Our sense of humor is often a coping mechanism when things get tough to help us deal with stress and anxiety. That's a good thing - it can help improve the mood, ours, and the mood of those around us, as well as increase resilience.

12. Surprising

ADHD can definitely keep us on our toes! One minute we're hyperfocusing on a project, and the next, we're completely distracted by riding bikes and we might find ourselves in a room not remembering why we're here. But you know what? That's one of the things that makes ADHD so awesome!

Sure, losing your wallet or forgetting your keys can be frustrating. Still, other times it leads to unexpected moments of creativity and inspiration. Plus, it's pretty cool to surprise ourselves and others with our abilities and ideas. Who knows what we'll come up with next? The possibilities are endless!

13. Best partner ever

Is your partner irritated by your tidying style? Well, it might be worth reminding them that people with ADHD know how to bring passion to a relationship.

When we fall in love, we fall hard and will do anything to make our partner feel loved and appreciated. Remember that generosity, empathy, and kindness we've just talked about? Well, they're all out. And with an intense focus, we can become completely absorbed in the romance, making our significant other feel like they are the center of the universe.

And don't get me started on creativity! Sure, we might forget our anniversary if we don't write it down, but the romantic types among us will want to do something unique to make our partner feel special.

Speaking of creativity...

14. Creativity

First, let's get one thing straight – Our imagination is limitless, and creativity is one of the hallmarks of ADHD. We see the world in our own special way. We make unusual connections. Our brains can work at an incredible pace, like a never-ending stream of consciousness.

Of course, we might daydream for hours - I spent my whole childhood daydreaming. As a result, we might find it difficult to stay focused on just one project or struggle to finish things because we're always coming up with new and exciting ideas. But if you can channel that energy and focus it into something productive, the results can be truly amazing.

15. Genius Thinking

All that creative way of thinking can simply lead to genius ideas and innovations. We may not always follow the traditional problem-solving paths, but we can come up with out-of-the-box solutions that others may have yet to consider.

Our brains are like little idea factories, churning out idea after idea with new and exciting thoughts coming out at lightning speed. It's like having a constant flow of inspiration that can be harnessed into something truly amazing. Paired with perseverance, our tendency to hyperfocus and stay laser-focused on a task until we've completed it to perfection, you can quickly see how it can lead to great things.

Once you know that, it is no surprise to hear that Leonardo Da Vinci and Albert Einstein are thought to have had ADHD.

It is important to keep in mind, though, that it takes time and effort to turn ADHD into a superpower. Biles didn't wake up a Gymnast, nor did Einstein spit out the E=MC2 as soon as he was born. It is a whole entire journey that requires patience and compassion for yourself. But guess what? I will show you how to develop that. First, we need to take care of our bodies and mind and we're going to explore the best ways to do that right now. So keep reading.

CHAPTER THREE

empowered body

5 WAYS TO HARNESS THE BODY-MIND CONNECTION

AFTER AN ADHD DIAGNOSIS, doctors often recommend making lifestyle changes alongside taking medication. Ever heard of the mind-body connection? Well, it's supported by decades of scientific research and the idea that our mental health impacts our bodies.

But guess what? The opposite is true, and our bodies' health significantly impacts our neuropsychiatry - known to you and I as our mental health and brain function.

Our bodies and minds are intimately connected, and how we treat one will inevitably affect the other. Show your body some love, and your brain will thank you. I'm not talking about being body-positive here, even though that's good for self-esteem. I mean: it is time to prioritize looking after our bodies as a radical act of self-care. So forget the bubble bath (for now) and let's look at what we eat.

1. FUEL FOR THOUGHT

First up, diet. Now, I could talk about this for days - in fact, I wrote a whole book about it. It's called *Brain-Boosting Food for Women with ADHD*, thanks for asking.

While ADHD isn't caused by diet, certain foods can worsen symptoms, while others can actually help. In fact, a review of thirty-five years of research published in *Clinical Pediatrics* found that "accumulated evidence suggests that a subgroup shows significant symptom improvement when consuming an AFC-free (Artificial food colors diet) diet and reacts with ADHD-type symptoms on challenge with AFCs. Of children with suspected sensitivities, 65% to 89% reacted when challenged with at least 100 mg of AFC." So the article suggests a trial elimination diet. So let's take a look.

WHAT TO AVOID?

Diet was the most impactful change I made to improve my brain function. Now I love a good donut as much as the next person, but there are some things we should avoid. Processed foods and sugar are at the top of the list. They may taste delicious but they can wreak havoc on our bodies and minds.

Processed Foods

Steer clear of processed foods. Why, you ask? Well, they're full of all sorts of nasties that can mess with your brain chemistry. Just to name a few:

- Artificial sweeteners can disrupt dopamine production.
- MSG has been linked to anxiety and depression, but that's been contested.
- Artificial food colors as we've just discussed are all the E numbers, E104, E122, E124, E131, E142 in the E.U and the UK. And they're called FD&C followed by a number in the U.S.

If that wasn't enough, these foods are usually high in sugar, which can cause a spike in blood sugar levels, leading to a temporary burst of energy followed by a crash. Let's take a closer look.

Sugar

Sorry to be the bearer of bad news, but if you have ADHD, you might want to think twice before indulging in too many sweet treats. I know, I know, I'm a killjoy, but hear me out.

Sugar can interfere with the production of serotonin. It's another transmitter that helps with mood regulation. So when we eat sugar, we experience a temporary boost in mood but crash harder later. It can lead to symptoms already often present alongside ADHD, like anxiety, depression, fatigue, and irritability.

But it's all about moderation; we aren't about a fad diet. So I'm not suggesting giving up sugar entirely. Treat yourself to cake, candies, or whatever sweet treats you like, but make sure they are just that: occasional treats and not a habit. And the one you really want to try to eliminate is all the hidden sugar in processed foods. If you want to add sweetness to a dish, try natural alternatives like honey or maple syrup.

So, if you want to keep your brain firing on all cylinders and avoid those pesky crashes, stick to whole, natural foods.

Intolerances

Some people have gluten, wheat, corn, soy, or dairy intolerances. But what does this have to do with ADHD? I'll tell you.

The link has been established by studies. More specifically, a study published in the *Journal of Attention Disorders* examined the association between ADHD and food sensitivities, including gluten and soy allergies. The researchers found that a subset of children with ADHD showed improvement in symptoms when following a gluten-free and/or soy-free diet. And if it's your case, cutting out certain foods can make a huge difference in how you feel and how well you can focus.

I mean, who wants to deal with brain fog and fidgety energy when they could be feeling clear-headed and ready to tackle the day? So if you suspect that certain foods are making your ADHD symptoms worse, it's definitely worth experimenting with an elimination diet. It's not as harsh as it sounds and can be done very simply:

1. Cut out just one ingredient from your diet entirely for one month and see if there's any improvement.
2. Eat a high dose of it with nothing else, for instance, a pint of milk or a plate of plain pasta, and note how you're feeling after.

Just be sure you check the labels, as what you're trying to avoid might be hiding in your favorite snack. You wouldn't believe how many types of chips contain milk [cue eye roll].

WHAT TO GO FOR?

"Okay, what can I eat then?" You might be asking moodily. I hear you. You're right - let's focus on the positive. In this case, it means focusing on what we should eat.

Proteins

Protein is a godsend for our brain function and regulation. Why? Because it is needed to produce the neurotransmitters we want. Remember our friends Dopamine and Norepinephrine? It also helps build and repair brain cells and provides energy for the brain. And if that wasn't enough, protein helps with hormone balance, too. What's not to like?

But before you rush to eat a whole cow, I need to add a word of caution. Not all proteins are equal. You want to stay clear of the ones high in saturated fat, like red meat, as many studies have shown that it can impair cognitive functions. So for inspiration, here are some excellent sources of lean protein:

- Poultry
- Fish
- Eggs
- Tofu
- Tempeh
- Seitan
- Beans and legumes

But here's the twist: it's not just about eating the recommended daily amount of protein; it's also about how we distribute it throughout the day.

You see, our bodies have this amazing ability to break down and utilize protein most effectively when it's consumed in smaller portions spread out across meals and snacks. By incorporating lean protein into our eating adventures throughout the day, we can maintain a steady supply of amino acids to support our brain function, ensuring a constant flow of nutrients to keep our ADHD brains on their toes.

This steady supply helps prevent the energy crashes and brain fog that can sometimes occur when we rely on large protein doses in just one or two meals. This has been a complete game-changer for me.

Healthy Fats

Let's talk about fat, baby! Okay, we've said a big no to saturated fat, but nearly 70% of our brain is made out of fat! Yep, seriously. And our brain needs healthy fat to function properly.

We've been so conditioned to think that fat is bad that it is hard to believe that some fats are good, but which ones? In short, omega 3! And here is a hand-picked selection of where you can find it:

- Fatty fish (think salmon, sardines, mackerel)
- Nuts and seeds
- Acai berries
- Avocado
- Seaweed
- Olive oil

So, are you ready to give fat the credit it deserves and include it in your diet?

Whole grain & rainbow

Now, onto whole grains and the rainbow of fruits and veggies. Not only are they delicious and colorful, but they also have tons of fiber.

Fiber is essential for balancing our blood sugar levels, which can greatly impact our mood.

So skip the refined carbs and opt for whole grains. Swap basmati rice for brown rice and regular pasta for whole wheat pasta. And remember to add a handful of veggies, like bell peppers, beets, and broccoli, along with it.

And for a sweet treat, you're spoiled with fiber-rich fruits like pineapples, mangos, and blueberries.

So let's fill our plates with a rainbow of delicious and fiber-rich foods to keep our brains and bodies happy! Here is some inspiration to get you started:

- Oats
- Whole wheat pasta
- Brown rice
- Buckwheat
- Quinoa
- Asparagus
- Bell peppers
- Beets
- Broccoli
- Cauliflower
- Leeks
- Onions
- Sweet potatoes
- Squash
- Pineapples
- Mangos
- Kiwi
- Honeydew melon
- Grapefruit
- Cantaloupe
- Blueberries are nicknamed
- Blackberries
- Cherries

SUPPLEMENTS

In an ideal world, we would get all the nutrients we need from our diet, but the world is not always ideal. So it might be useful at times to give our brain function a helping hand to improve symptoms.

Here are some worth considering to help manage ADHD symptoms:

- Omega 3 is the superstar supplement for the ADHD brain. It's like the Robin to your Batman brain, swooping in to save the day with its anti-inflammatory powers and brain-boosting benefits. It's the good fat we're chasing in food.
- Ashwagandha is part of ancient Ayurvedic medicine and is known as "Indian Ginseng." This herb is all about balance and harmony. It is best known for relieving stress and giving you an energy boost. It also supports cognitive functions like focus and memory.
- Zinc is a little mineral powerhouse. It is like a tiny shield that protects your brain from harm while giving you a little boost of energy.
- Vitamin D is sunshine in a bottle. So if you don't get enough sunlight, it might be an interesting option to help your brain function.
- Ginkgo Biloba: It can help boost blood flow and oxygen to our brain. The result? It can help with focus, make sure we can think clearly, and stay sharp.

I've got to add the traditional word of caution here. Supplementing is not a replacement for medication, and you're certainly wise enough to know that you should talk to a medical professional before starting a new supplement.

2. WASH IT DOWN

It's not all about food! We are also all the liquid that goes into our body. So let's have a look at drinks.

WATER

Let's start with the self-explanatory one!

I'm sure you know this already, but it's always worth remembering-water is crucial for our brain function. And on the flip side, dehydration can have a devastating effect on our brain cells and impact how they communicate.

Hands up if sometimes you hyperfocus so hard on something you forget to drink. Yep, I've been there, too. So that's why I want to hammer home the point that you must prioritize staying hydrated. Here are a few tricks that have helped me.

Bottle it

Keep a water bottle nearby. Seeing it reminds us to do it even in the height of hyperfocus when getting up to fill a cup is off the table. Water bottles make it easier to track the amount we drink, too.

Spice it up

You can spice up your hydration game without adding sugar by infusing your water with flavorful ingredients like lemon, cucumber, or mint. Just drop it in that water bottle. It will look pretty, too.

Make it hot

Consider drinking non-caffeinated warm beverages during the cold months. Herbal teas like rosemary, sage, and lemon balm are known to enhance memory and focus. Or, to be honest, I often just drink hot water. Call me weird, but it's okay, I can take it.

Track it

Use the daily planner I've made for you to track how much you drink throughout the day. The daily recommended intake is about eight glasses. So every time you down one, color one of those little glasses. Of course, the amount you need will vary depending on the weather and your physical activity.

Gamify it

If you like to gamify life a bit, you can track your water intake with an app. You can simply use a habit tracker, or there are some special apps for it out there, of course! "My Hydration" and "Drink Water" are both simple free options as I type these words. If you're more of an analog kind of girl, draw a little glass in your journal whenever you down a glass (of water, wine doesn't count).

COFFEE

Ah, coffee…

This is a hotly debated topic in the ADHD community, with many people using it as a way to self-medicate before their diagnosis. I'm definitely on the addict side, but I've heard fellow ADHDers say it makes them sleepy.

Caffeine is a stimulant that can boost dopamine levels, improve concentration, and even help with mood and depression. No wonder so many of us like it. But it has some serious downsides, such as anxiety, restlessness, headaches, and insomnia.

The recommended daily maximum amount of caffeine is 400mg, around 5 cups of coffee. However, please experiment with this yourself to figure out what works best for you. I limit myself to four cups and never drink caffeine after lunchtime. Here are a few pros and cons so you can battle it out yourself:

Pros:

- It's a stimulant, so it boosts dopamine.
- It can help with concentration and focus.
- It can help with mood and depression.
- It can promote alertness.

Cons:

- It can cause anxiety and jitters.
- It can make you feel restless or agitated.

- It can trigger headaches.
- It can interfere with sleep and cause insomnia.

So have a think and decide how much coffee you should have and when you should drink it.

GREEN TEA

Green tea, particularly matcha, can be a great alternative to coffee. It's packed with antioxidants and has a metabolism-boosting effect similar to coffee. It contains caffeine too, about 30-50 mg per cup. That's about two to three times less than coffee. Its true superpower comes from theanine, an amino acid found in tea leaves and some mushrooms, which can help you relax and focus simultaneously.

By the way, black tea has theanine too, but a lot less than green tea and a lot more caffeine. So once again, see what you prefer and make sure it is enjoyable too!

3. MOVE IT

Okay, I need to state the obvious again, but movement is key to improving ADHD symptoms. It is the number one recommendation for lifestyle changes when you go through a diagnosis or even just look at recommendations online. But there are many ways in which we can add physical activities to our life, and I'm here to give you pointers and help you figure out the ones that work for you.

EXERCISING

Well, duh! But why is exercising good for our brains? Well, research shows that when you exercise, your brain releases dopamine, which helps with focus and attention.

A particular study published in the *Journal of Attention Disorders* involved 32 children with ADHD who participated in a 10-week exercise program. And guess what? In the end, the children showed significant improvements in their ability to concentrate, follow directions, and control impulsive behaviors. They also showed improvements in their overall social behavior and self-esteem.

And the magic of it is that exercise has other mental health benefits, too! It reduces stress and anxiety, boosts self-esteem, and improves mood. And it's got a cumulative effect, too, so the more you keep at it, the bigger its impact.

And if you can exercise outdoors, that's even better, because there is evidence from a national study published in the *American Journal of Public Health* that spending time in natural outdoor settings reduces ADHD symptoms.

Joyful Movement

Discovering the exercise that brings you joy is essential because you want to keep at it. Plus, joy = extra dopamine, so double-win!

If hitting the gym thrice a week for 45 minutes works for you, brilliant! Keep at it. But if you are like me and dislike exercising because it becomes dull, try tricking your brain with a fun activity that doesn't feel like exercising. You can get creative and social or make it an adventure! It could look like this:

- Group sport
- Indoor climbing
- Hula hoops
- Surfing
- Pole dancing
- Drumming
- Ballroom dancing
- Hiking with the family
- Bike ride
- Tennis with a friend
- Boxing
- Kayaking
- Bowling with friends

YOGA

No chapter on ADHD and the mind-body connection would be complete without discussing yoga. It is the ultimate way to get your mind and body in sync! But it's not just hype, there are some good reasons why it is recommended time and time again.

Biological/neurological benefits

Yoga has been shown to increase levels of GABA, a neurotransmitter that helps regulate anxiety and stress. It can also increase gray matter in the brain, which is associated with improved cognitive function and memory.

Mental benefits

Yoga can help quiet the mind and improve focus. It can also increase empathy and reduce stress and anxiety.

Physical benefits

Like other types of exercise, yoga can help increase energy levels and improve overall physical fitness. So it's a great way to get moving and get your blood flowing, but it can be much more gentle than a spin class.

There are many different types of yoga, from very still to very energetic, so try out different classes to see what works for you. And if you're worried about the cost of yoga classes, don't be! There are plenty of free resources to choose from, including apps and YouTube videos. I love the app called Down Dog. It's super easy to follow, and you can customize your practice type, time, and level.

NEAT

NEAT stands for Non-Exercise Activity Thermogenesis, a fancy way of saying "the energy you use doing stuff that isn't exercise."

Basically, NEAT is all about moving your body in little ways throughout the day. It's not about sweating it out at the gym or doing a 5k every morning. No, no, no. NEAT is all about finding little opportunities to move more.

And the best part? By moving more throughout the day, you can improve your mood, reduce stress and anxiety, and even boost your creativity.

Here are a few things you can do to incorporate NEAT into your day-to-day:

- Add more walking into your daily routine: park further away when going to work or take a lunchtime walk.
- Opt for taking the stairs instead of the elevator.
- Take a dance break at lunchtime, or have a 10-minute kitchen dance party to unwind after work.
- Cycle to work and enjoy the fresh air.
- Use a standing desk: standing while working can help you move more and help reduce feelings of restlessness.
- Sit on an exercise ball either as a desk chair or at home. It can also help you engage your core and improve your posture.
- Pace: try pacing when you're on the phone, brainstorming ideas, or waiting for the bus.
- Do some stretches at your desk to break up long periods of sitting.
- Try some chair yoga exercises to relieve stress and tension.
- Play a game of frisbee with your kids after school.
- Run for the bus!
- Do some housework - a lot more on this later.

FIDGETING

Do you fidget? A lot of people with ADHD tend to. Fidgeting is basically any small, repetitive movement that you do, like tapping your foot, drumming your fingers, or twirling a pen.

You might well have been told off for fidgeting as a child or even these days because it is seen as a sign of restlessness. But for us, it can actually be a helpful tool. Here's why:

Helps stay focused

These small repetitive movements can provide just enough stimulation to keep your brain engaged without distracting you from the task at hand.

Relieves stress and anxiety

It gives your body an outlet for that restless energy and can help you feel more calm and centred.

Improves memory

You read that right! Turns out fidgeting can improve working memory in people with ADHD. If you're fidgeting while trying to memorize something, it can help your brain retain that information better.

So, if you feel like fidgeting, don't feel bad about it! Obviously, you want to be aware of the world around you, as your fidgeting to focus might distract someone else. But generally speaking, embrace it! That could be one of your unmasking steps.

4. SLEEP IS NOT FOR THE WEAK

So, here's the deal: people with ADHD tend to have trouble sleeping, and it's not just because we have too many thoughts bouncing around in our heads. Nope, it's also a biological thing. You see, our executive functions that deal with things like organization and impulse control are often impaired and struggle with winding down.

Sleep disorders can come in different shapes and forms. It can be insomnia, sleep apnea, or restless leg syndrome. It might be that you have trouble falling asleep, or it might be that you wake up in the middle of the night or too early! And not getting enough sleep sucks. It can really mess with your head. It can make you even more forgetful and unfocused than usual, and it can simply but annoyingly make you feel pretty darn cranky.

FALLING ASLEEP

If you have trouble falling asleep, there are lots of things you can do.

Keep a regular sleep schedule

That's the first thing you'll hear, and it sounds boring, but try it out. Go to bed and wake up at the same time every day, even on the weekends (which, let's be real, is easier said than done).

That's why I've included a bedtime and a wake-up time in your Bedtime Planner. It's part of your Empowered ADHD Planners Pack. If you haven't downloaded it yet, go to: bit.ly/ EmpoweredPlanners

Avoid screens before bed

The recommendation is usually to switch off from screens (yes, Netflix, too) at least 30 minutes before going to bed. And don't even think about doing work or anything else that requires hyperfocus right before bedtime. Put that phone down; you're just asking for trouble.

Get enough daylight

Try to spend some time outside if you can. And if you're really struggling with dark, gray, miserable winters, you might want to consider light therapy.

Bedroom is for sleeping

Keep your bedroom (or bed, if you live in one room) for sleeping. Oh, and, you know, sex if you feel like it. Don't use it as a work-space or anything like that; otherwise, your brain will start associating bed with work.

Experiment with diet

Certain foods and drinks can make things worse, so pay attention to how you feel after you eat or drink certain things (I'm looking at you, alcohol).

Listen to relax

Listen to calming music or guided meditations to help relax your mind and body before bed. You can find a lot of free resources. I've got two favorite ones. Endel, which has a soundscape for everything, including sleep. And Insight Timer, which is a meditation app with a huge choice of sleep meditation.

Know your senses

If you get sensory overload in the daytime, it might also affect you at night. So you might want to try blackout curtains or a sleep mask to convince your brain it's nighttime. You can also try earplugs if noise bothers you or a weighted blanket to help you feel more secure and relaxed. More on sensory sensitivity, a bit later in this chapter.

PROTEINS · Supplements · Healthy FATS · WHOLE GRAINS & Rainbow

· EXERCISE · JOYFUL MOVEMENT ·
· N.E.A.T · FIDGETING · SLEEP ·

But what if the problem is not dozing off at night but waking up at 4 am with racing thoughts and anxiety?

Well, first, all of the above can help as they will prepare you for a good *full* night's sleep. But here are a few extra tips that can help.

Notepad and pen

Keep a notepad and pen near your bed and write down any tasks or thoughts that have popped into your racing mind in the middle of the night. Once on paper, you can let them go, knowing you will be able to pick them up tomorrow morning.

Gratitude list

Make a mental gratitude list by reminding yourself of all the things you're thankful for in your life. It's a great way to shift your focus to the positive things instead of stressing about the negative. We'll look at this in more detail in the next chapter.

Pat-on-the-back list

Same idea, but the list celebrates all the little accomplishments from the day before. It's like giving yourself a mental high-five! And again, more details to come in the next chapter.

Headphones

Keep headphones near your bed and listen to a sleeping meditation to help you go back to sleep.

Crafting a bedtime routine is key, and we will take a deeper dive into the techniques that can help your mind wind down before bed in the next chapter.

5. ALL THE SENSES

Sensory processing is a delicate dance between your brain and the world around you. But in the ADHD world, that dance can sometimes feel a little out of sync. It can take different forms for different people, but sensory problems are often one of those things that people discover later, like, "Oh, that's because of ADHD?"

TYPES OF SENSORY PROBLEMS

There are a lot of different sensory problems out there, but they're broadly divided into three categories.

Hypersensitivity

Hypersensitivity to sensory input, also known as sensory over-responsivity, is when we have an exaggerated and intense response to sensory stimuli in our environment. It's like having sensory bionic powers that are turned up to the highest level.

Hyposensitivity

That's basically the opposite. Hyposensitivity to sensory input, also known as sensory under-responsivity, is when we have a decreased or muted response to sensory stimuli in our environment. It's like wearing noise-canceling headphones or living in a bubble that filters out certain sensory information.

Sensory integration

Difficulty with sensory integration is like you're being thrown a million balls all at once and you're expected to keep them all up in the air. The brain struggles to sort out which sensory input is what and comfortably processes them. It can make engaging in daily activities really tricky.

And, of course, you can have a mix of it all! You might be the ultimate detective, picking up on details that others miss. But other times, it's like your senses go on vacation, and you barely notice the world around you. "What can I do about it? Heeeelp!" You might be screaming in your head. Well, before we look at tools, let's take a closer look at some common symptoms.

Needless to say that these experiences can vary from person to person, but here are some sensations you might find familiar.

Sound Symphony

Do you ever get really irritated by the noise of the air-con in a meeting? Or do you feel like a buzzing fly can turn into a full-blown concert in your head? Yes, noise sensitivity is a common sensory symptom among adults with ADHD. It's like having your volume dial set to hypersensitive mode, making everyday sounds feel like a racket.

Texture Tango

You know those tags on clothes that feel like mini torture devices? Or that one fabric that sends shivers down your spine? Well, welcome to the world of texture sensitivity, another classic for people with ADHD. It's like your skin has its own opinions about what it likes and dislikes, and it can be quite vocal about it.

Visual Distractions

If a room has a screen, do you find it impossible to ignore? Of course, there are also bright lights and flashy signs. It's like your attention is drawn to every shiny object in the room, and you need extra effort to filter out the visual noise and stay focused.

Smell Surprise

Ah, the power of scents. While some people may enjoy a pleasant fragrance, for adults with ADHD, certain smells can feel like a sensory overload. Strong perfumes, scented cleaning products, or even a spicy dish cooking in the kitchen can trigger a sensory frenzy, making it hard to focus on anything else.

Taste Trigger

There is very little research on taste sensitivity. However, a study at Duke University has established a link between picky eating and ADHD. Eating can be a full-on experience for anyone with heightened sensitivity. There are the textures, the smells, the visual cues, and, don't get me started with sounds! Many people with ADHD report suffering from misophonia and being particularly triggered by the sound of eating.

Oh dear, I feel overwhelmed just mentioning all of those. So the next (and exciting) question is: what can we do about it? Well, let's take a look.

TRIGGERS AND ENVIRONMENT

Identify triggers

First things first, let's become trigger detectives. Pay close attention to those sneaky things that set off your sensory fireworks. Is it certain sounds, bright lights, or scratchy fabrics? Jot it down in your journal, or just create a list on your phone. Write down all the sensory triggers you notice as you go about your life.

Once you've identified your arch-nemeses, you can start devising your brilliant plans.

Mwa ha ha!!!

Modify the environment

Modify the environment, my friends! Take charge and create a sensory-friendly oasis. It doesn't have to be costly or complicated. It can be as simple as dimming the lights or giving underwear a miss.

I asked a group of women with ADHD for their go-to sensory hacks, and here is a list of what they came up with. Try one, try them all, and see what works for you:

- Cut out clothing labels and tags.
- Stick to natural fabric.
- Forget underwear or invest in high-waisted 'granny' ones.
- Use ankle socks or roll the top of normal socks.
- Lose the high heels and stick to comfy shoes or go bare feet at home.
- Use lip balms.
- Use hand cream.

- Wear rubber gloves to do the dishes.
- Keep your nails short.
- Use a hair tie.
- Use sunglasses.
- Invest in earplugs, ear defenders, or noise-canceling headphones.
- Listen to music, try binaural beats and ASMR.
- Open the windows to get rid of irritating smells.

But if those hacks are not enough, or if you're already doing those, there are some very helpful strategies you can try. Let's check them out now.

Coping Strategies

Once you've changed what you could in your environment, you might want to incorporate these coping strategies.

Mindfulness and Meditation

We're going to talk about mindfulness exercises and meditation techniques right in the next chapter. For now, just know that they can be very useful tools to help with sensory awareness and regulate our responses to sensory stimulation. So that's another reason to incorporate them into your life.

Take Sensory Breaks

Identify a quiet space at home and at work where you can take yourself when you get overstimulated. Take a few minutes to close your eyes and take a few deep breaths. If you have identified a particular moment in the day when it all becomes a bit too much, then you could turn it into a preventative routine and visit your calming spot before getting overwhelmed.

Grounding Techniques

Grounding techniques can help bring your attention back to the present moment and provide a sense of stability. Here are a few quick ones you can try without going full-on meditation:

- Focus on your breath.
- Feel your feet on the ground.
- Focus on a sensory object like a stress ball, a stone, or anything you like the texture of.
- Acknowledge 5 things you can see, 4 things you can touch, 3 things you can hear, 2 things you can smell, and 1 thing you can taste.

SENSORY DIET

That's usually done with an occupational therapist and personalized to your needs. If it's something you'd like to explore further, it would be a good idea to talk to your health practitioner about it. Everything we have just mentioned about movement will help, but here are a few more things you could try.

Deep Pressure

You could invest in a weighted blanket or compression clothes. Also, try hugging a pillow or squeezing stress balls.

Oral Sensory Activities

You could try chewing gum or chewable necklaces to provide oral sensory input. Drinking through a straw can also be a fun way to introduce oral stimulation.

Visual Regulation

Creating a visually organized and clutter-free environment can help. We will look at how we can do that in chapter 6. Pair it with visual organization tools like color-coded schedules or checklists to provide structure and reduce sensory overwhelm.

And don't hesitate to go for the rockstar look and start wearing tinted glasses. You can also try wearing a hat or visor to reduce visual glare or brightness.

Auditory Regulation

When it comes to audio sensitivity, you have two choices: make it quieter or replace the noise. Both can be helpful depending on the circumstances, so play with both.

Try listening to calming or ambient music or nature sounds through headphones. My personal favorite is rain. The world is full of free and paying apps for that. TickTick has some, but I often search for tracks on Spotify.

On the other hand, consider investing in noise-canceling headphones or earplugs for noisy or overstimulating environments.

Tactile Sensory Activities

Exploring texture and keeping your hands busy can help with sensory regulation and body awareness, which lower stress and promote attention and focus.

Fidgeting is good for you, remember? So while you might not be able to play with kinetic sand in a work meeting, you might be able to hold a stone, rub a fabric you like, or maybe even knit.

Scent-Based Activities

Try calming essential oils or scented candles like lavender or chamomile. If you like them, turn them into an anchor by lighting them when it is time to relax. Soon you'll start associating this scent with relaxation.

The key is to be aware of your own sensory sensitivities, embrace your quirks, and find strategies that work for you. Whether it's creating a calm and sensory-friendly environment, using tools to manage distractions, wearing comfy clothes, or incorporating movement breaks into your routine. Check which strategies make your senses shout, "Hooray!"

CHAPTER FOUR

empowered brain

15 STRATEGIES TO SLOW DOWN YOUR RACING THOUGHTS

ARE you tired of your mind racing at a million miles per hour, leaving you feeling overwhelmed? Do you wish you could wave a magic wand to switch off the constant chatter in your brain? You're not alone. I completely understand the feeling, and so do most women with ADHD.

The good news is, we don't need a magic wand! I mean, sure, it would make life easier, but we can still calm our internal noise without it. In fact, I have gathered 15 powerful tools and proven strategies you can use to slow down those racing thoughts and improve your overall mental well-being.

Ready to ditch the worry loops? Follow me!

1. POSITIVE AFFIRMATIONS

I know, I know, it does sound like some new-age, hippy mumbo jumbo. And although you could argue that I probably look like a hippy to some people, I was very skeptical at first, too. That was until I gave it a proper shot and noticed it was instantly bringing my anxiety down.

And you don't need to take my word for it because science backs me up on that one.

Many studies, including one conducted at Carnegie Mellon University in 2013, have proven that positive affirmations can reduce stress and negative self-talk. "So what are we waiting for?" you're now asking. Well, let me guide you.

So first, you want to choose an affirmation that resonates with you. It could be something simple like, "I am capable" or "I am worthy of love and respect." Write it down in your daily planner. You know, the one I've included in your planners pack. If you still need to get it, you can find it here: bit.ly/EmpoweredPlanners.

Writing it down will help solidify it in your mind, but you also need to say it to yourself multiple times throughout the day. You can even set a reminder on your phone to make sure you're doing it at certain times.

But here's the thing - it's not just about reciting a phrase like a robot. Say it like you mean it. Are you cringing yet? It's totally normal. With practice, you'll start to feel more in alignment with it, and it will become a powerful tool in your mental health toolkit.

Are you ready to give it a try? Make sure you stick with the affirmation you've picked for at least a week. Here are some specially selected affirmations you can pick from:

- I choose to be happy.
- My life is taking place right here, right now.
- I rise above negative feelings.
- I am focusing on positive thoughts.
- I am resilient, strong, and brave.
- *I* decide how *I* feel.
- When I lie down to sleep, everything is as it should be, and I rest content.
- I am in charge of my thoughts, and I accept myself.
- These are just thoughts.
- I breathe, I am collected, and I am calm.
- This is just one moment in time.
- This is one isolated moment, not my entire life.
- I embrace my feelings.
- I have come this far, and I am proud of myself.

- I am on a journey, ever growing and developing.
- I embrace the present moment with gratitude
- I am free of others' judgment; I totally accept myself.
- I accept and love myself thoroughly and completely.
- I am liberating myself from fear, judgment, and doubt.
- I do my very best, and that's great.
- I am resilient and can handle problems with expertise.
- I am enough.
- I have everything I need to deal with this.

Once you get used to it and enjoy using affirmations, you might want to start crafting your own. Go ahead! Just make sure the affirmation focuses on you, so use "I" statements, and make it in the present tense.

2. DAILY TREAT

Did someone say "daily treat?" Okay, wipe that chocolate cake off your mind. Not that kind of treat; remember the last chapter? But there are other ways to give yourself a mini celebration every day. And let's be real, who doesn't love a little celebration? "Ceeeeeeelebraaaate good times, come on! Ooh, ooh, ooh, ooh"

And actually, singing along to Kool & The Gang can totally be your daily treat. It doesn't have to be an extravagant thing or take up too much of your day, just something that makes you happy and gives you a little dopamine boost. Write it down in your daily planner, and look forward to it.

Maybe you love the taste of a special coffee or enjoy listening to a certain podcast on your commute. Whatever it is, make it a part of your daily routine to pick an intentional moment of joy. Think of it as a little gift to yourself for making it through another day.

Even just taking a few minutes to do something you enjoy can make a big difference in your mental well-being. So go ahead, treat yourself!

3. Switch-Off

Give your brain a well-deserved break and switch off from social media, at least for a while. It's worth it. Seriously. Did you know that research, such as the study published in the journal *Cyberpsychology, Behavior, and Social Networking*, has shown that people with ADHD are more likely to experience negative effects from social media use, like anxiety and depression?

But don't worry, it doesn't have to be forever. See it as hitting the reset button. That same study and many others have shown that taking a break, even as short as one week, can improve mental well-being and decrease anxiety.

"Okay, I'll switch off!" I hear you cry, "But how?" Fear not, here are five steps you can take to break up with your phone:

1. Assess the situation

First things first, check how much time you spend on social media and how it makes you feel. If it's making you feel down or anxious, then it's probably time to dial it down.

2. Identify the problem

Next, check whether it is just certain platforms or certain people. Unfollow or mute people who make you feel like a failure. You don't need that negativity in your life!

Instead, surround yourself with positive, uplifting, and inspiring content. This can be a work in progress, and you can review it regularly.

3. Social with a cause

Stop the mindless scrolling and use social media for a purpose. Maybe it's to check in with a supportive ADHD group or to catch up with a friend. And when you're done, switch off and move on to something else. You can even put a timer on to limit yourself if you need to.

4. Serious measures

If you find it hard to resist the urge to scroll, try deleting the app from your phone. You can still check it on your computer or other devices, but you won't have it at your fingertips all the time.

5. The hardcore method

If you're feeling all in, you can even delete your account altogether!

You can also take physical measures like leaving your phone out of sight while working or in the evening. If you don't need to be on call, try switching your phone off an hour before bed and delay switching it on in the morning.

Remember, it's okay to take small steps at first. Start by dialing it down and see how it makes you feel.

4. Take your Creativity out for a Play

Creativity gets you in a state of flow. Do you know what I mean? It's that magical state where you're completely absorbed into what you're doing and experience a deep sense of enjoyment.

Sure, it sounds a lot like hyperfocus, but the difference is that a state of flow allows you to process thoughts and emotions. It's kind of free therapy. You're relaxing without even trying, and it works wonders to reduce stress and anxiety.

It works best with activities that won't engage your brain too much, so think of all things needle-related and craft in general, and of course, drawing, painting, or even coloring books. You can practice on your own, take an online course, or join a local group or class.

5. Write it Down

I know what you're thinking, "But I don't have time for writing!" Hear me out, though. You're freeing up mental space by getting all those thoughts out of your head and onto paper. You're no longer trying to hold onto everything in your mind, which is obviously an overwhelming task. Trying to remember everything you have to do, plus processing the sensory information overload, is a huge challenge.

So, here are five simple ways of writing thoughts that can help:

1. To-do lists

They can be beneficial for organizing tasks and prioritizing what needs to get done. By writing down everything you need to do, you can break it down into manageable steps and create an action plan. Then you can stop worrying about them.

2. Calendars

They are an absolute must for scheduling appointments and events and ensuring you don't forget anything important.

3. Taking notes

Have you ever had lots of brilliant ideas about the new thing you're hyper-fixating on, but you can't do anything about it because it's not the right time and you're meant to do something else, like, you know, work? Take notes! It will free your mind, and you will be able to pick it up later.

So jot down ideas, thoughts, and reminders whether you're using your phone or a notebook. And, an extra perk: writing something down can help you remember it later.

4. Planners

They are a bit of a hybrid, and you can find planners for everything. In the Empowered ADHD Planners Pack, I've included three which I think are essential: a daily planner, a bedtime planner, and a budget planner. You know where to find them, right? bit.ly/ EmpoweredPlanners

I've designed them to help you use important tools in this book. But as you're using them and start to identify what techniques work best for you, feel free to spread your wings and design your own. Something a bullet journal can be helpful for.

5. Bullet journal

It was my (not so) secret weapon pre-smartphone. It is a customizable way to track your thoughts, ideas, and progress toward your goals. You don't have to make it as fancy as what social media tells you, but you can if it helps you relax.

People use it as a to-do list, habit tracker, way of remembering happy moments, and so much more. But instead of writing lengthy journal pages, it takes the form of bullet points, hence the name.

6. Journaling

Actually, journaling is a tool in itself.

6. JOURNALING

Journaling is like having a secret conversation with yourself that only you get to see. But the benefits are far from being a private place to express your thoughts. It's a tool that can help you slow down your thoughts, dig deeper and understand yourself better. It's like a therapy session without the awkward silence and price tag.

You can use journaling to identify patterns and triggers in your life. By being honest with yourself and writing it down, you can start to see what's working and what's not. You can also analyze and rephrase failures and/or fears, which you can turn into positive affirmations. It's like a brain dump, but with a purpose.

Now, the question is, by hand or by app? Writing by hand has its perks; it helps you physically slow down, and who doesn't get excited about quality stationery? Going to buy a notebook can even be one of your daily treats! It's like having a little moment of joy every time you pick up that special pen and open your notebook. Size matters; make sure you choose a size big enough to write comfortably but small enough to fit into your bag. A5 (8.8" x 5.5") is my personal favorite.

On the other hand, apps can be more exciting and they're always in your pocket, so you can journal anywhere, anytime. Plus, some apps have cool features like daily prompts and reminders to keep you motivated. Many of them also let you add other media, like photos, or dictate instead of writing. If you're into digital, check Day One, Daylio, 5 Minute Journal, and Grid Diary.

So, whether you prefer the traditional pen and paper or the convenience of technology, there's a journaling method for everyone.

7. GRATITUDE LIST

A gratitude list is one of the most efficient techniques you could add to your journal, and that's why I've added it to your bedtime planner.

It's super simple, really. All you have to do is write down ten things you're grateful for at the end of each day. They can be anything - from the big stuff, like getting a promotion or having a great date, to the little things, like seeing a beautiful sunset, eating your favorite snack, or the bus arriving on time.

Now, I know what you're thinking: "Ten things?! That's a lot!" But trust me, that's where the magic happens. That's how you learn to push past the obvious ones, and the mental transformation happens. Don't worry; the more you do it, the easier it gets.

Not only does it help you focus on the positive, but it actually trains your brain to seek out those little moments of joy throughout the day. And guess what those little joys get you? That's right, nice dopamine boosts!

So go ahead, and give it a try. Put a notebook beside your bed, set a reminder on your phone, and start including a gratitude list in your bedtime routine.

8. PAT-ON-THE-BACK LIST

Self-compassion is not just about saying nice things to yourself and putting on a happy face - it's about really showing yourself some love and kindness. And what better way to do that than with what I call a "pat-on-the-back list."

That's another one I've added to your planner. This list is like a little love letter to yourself. Write down all the things you've accomplished today, big and small, and give yourself a virtual pat on the back. Did you finally finish that project that's been looming over you? Did you remember to take your ADHD medication today? Did you make yourself a delicious and nutritious meal? Yes, you did! And you deserve recognition for it.

I am a master champion of looking at my to-do list and seeing all the things I haven't done (yet). And even when I tick things off my list, I forget all the 'little' things I take for granted. You know the ones I mean: cooking, getting the kids to school on time, washing my hair. Celebrating our accomplishments, even the little ones, is important because it helps us build confidence and self-esteem.

So take a moment to reflect on your achievements, big and small, make that pat-on-the-back list, and give yourself a well-deserved round of applause.

9. BED-TIME ROUTINE

A peak time for racing thoughts is when we lay in bed to fall asleep. And that's totally understandable and normal. This is because, for many people with ADHD, that's the only moment we're not busy doing something, so our brain can finally get a chance to process all those thoughts. Think of it like a very full hard drive creating a backup.

So, for that reason, it is super important to have a good bedtime routine. One great way to slow down those racing thoughts is to incorporate some of the tools we've just discussed. Journaling, a gratitude list, and a pat-on-the-back list are all great to add to your bedtime routine.

The bedtime planner helps you create a frame for that backup. So, you know those planners you downloaded at the beginning of the book? Print them out and start using them. When it's time to go to bed, jot down some things you are grateful for today.

It is also time to revisit the techniques we've explored in Chapter 3 about falling asleep and craft the bedtime routine that works for you. What time are you going to switch off from screens? Are you going to include meditation?

Speaking of meditation, it doesn't have to be a bedtime activity only. Let's take a closer look.

10. MEDITATION

So meditation is one of the most effective ways to calm racing thoughts in people with ADHD? How? Well, meditation helps to calm the mind and increase focus by training the brain to be more present and, therefore, less distracted.

Okay, you're thinking: "And here is some hippy nonsense again." Are you? Well, think again. Just 10 minutes of meditation per day can help reduce anxiety and depression significantly. That claim comes from a study published in the *Journal of Attention Disorders* that investigated the effects of daily meditation on adults with ADHD.

And here's another good news: there are different types of meditation, so you can pick what works best for you! If you're unsure where to start, you can find many of them on Insight Timer, a free app. Here are seven types you might like to explore:

1. Guided visualization meditation

An excellent starting point if you've never practiced. It usually takes you through a scenario, so it is well suited to an imaginative ADHD mind.

2. Body scan meditation

It takes you through your whole body and it is very helpful to ground yourself when you're going through racing thoughts. You can do it yourself or listen to someone guide you.

3.Loving-Kindness meditation

It can really help lift the mood by making you focus on well-wishes for yourself and others.

4. Transcendental meditation

A little bit more tricky for a busy mind. Focus on a mantra or a sound and gently bring your attention back when your mind drifts off.

5. Yoga meditation

Yoga practice is a form of meditation as you focus on your body and breathing. It also often involves a 'savasana' where your body is at rest, and you become aware of your inner self.

6. Breathing meditation

It can be part of a yoga practice too. For this type, you're using your breathing as an anchor for your mind. We're going to look at breathing exercises in a short while.

7. Mindfulness meditation

There has been a lot of research on the benefits of mindfulness meditation for people with ADHD. So we're going to take a closer look at it right now.

Meditation can be a spa day for your brain! No cucumber slices needed. Just pick one to try and close your eyes.

II. MINDFULNESS

Mindfulness is another classic recommendation for people with ADHD, including from Psychiatrists. And for good reasons! If you're not receptive to anything sounding vaguely spiritual, fret not, there is proof. A study published in the *Journal of Attention Disorders* has shown that only eight weeks of mindfulness practice can improve the symptoms of adults with ADHD, particularly attention and impulsivity.

What I particularly like about mindfulness is that this is something to infuse in your life rather than an extra activity to add to your to-do list. It's about focusing on what you're doing and being present in the moment. So eating becomes mindful eating, a walk in nature becomes a mindful walk, a run becomes a mindful run... you get the idea. Talking of running, the Nike Run Club app has some mindful runs, and it's free.

Here are a few tips to help you turn any activity into a mindful one.

Become a sensory detective

Pay attention to all your senses. Are you feeling hot or cold? How does the air or fabric feel on your skin? What smell can you identify? What are the background noises?

Become an emotion detective

Ask yourself: How am I feeling? What is the primary feeling? Any other feelings there?

Become an observer

Take notes of those sensations and feelings with a curious but non-judgemental mind.

If you're keen to dive deeper, try the book *The Mindfulness Prescription for Adult ADHD: An 8-Step Program for Strengthening Attention, Managing Emotions, and Achieving Your Goals.* Another good choice is Headspace, the go-to app for mindfulness practice. It's not free, but it could be a great investment if you think mindfulness is right for you.

12. Breathing Exercises and Techniques

As we've just discussed, breathing can be a meditation practice. It is also one of those emergency tools you can pull out of your toolbox when everything feels just too overwhelming. And the best part? It's free, and you can do it anywhere, anytime! By simply focusing on your breathing for a couple of minutes, you can get (almost literally) life-saving results:

Regain control

By taking deep breaths, you can help calm the nervous system, which can help you feel calmer, more grounded, and relieve stress and anxiety.

Improve focus

Breathing deeply increases the oxygen flow to the brain, which helps with focus and concentration.

Slow the racing thoughts

By focusing on your breathing, you're becoming more self-aware, which promotes clarity and helps manage emotions.

Now, if you want to make sure you can rip all those benefits when you need them the most, the trick is to practice when you don't, even just for a couple of minutes. But try to do it daily. So here are a few exercises to get you started:

Box breathing

- breath in for four seconds
- hold your breath for four seconds
- exhale for four seconds
- hold your breath for four seconds again.

Think that you're creating a square (a box) with four equal sides of four. This can help regulate your breathing and calm your mind.

4-7-8 breathing

- breathing in for four seconds
- holding your breath for seven seconds
- exhaling for eight seconds

It's a bit of a longer hold on the exhale, but it can help relax your body and mind.

Lion's breath

- Taking a deep breath in through your nose
- Exhaling forcefully while sticking out your tongue and making a "ha" sound.

It may look a bit silly, but this technique can help release tension in your face and throat and promote relaxation.

Remember, it's important to practice these techniques every day, even when you're not feeling overwhelmed, so they become second nature when you need them the most.

13. Sophrology

I know it might sound like a fancy French pastry, but it's actually a relaxation technique that's gaining popularity. It's like mindfulness but with some oomph compared to Mindfulness-Based Stress Reduction (MBSR). It feels more dynamic and interactive, which may sound appealing to the ADHD brain.

Sophrology combines relaxation, breathing exercises, gentle movements, visualization, and the sound of the voice. It helps individuals reach a dynamic relaxation state, which is different from just being calm or mindful.

If you're looking for something a little more on the dynamic side, this could be the perfect fit for you. Dominique Antiglio's book, *The Life-Changing Power of Sophrology,* is a good starting point.

If you're curious, try both MBSR and Sophrology and see which one resonates with you.

14. Yoga Nidra

Ahhh... I feel relaxed just hearing those two words. I don't know why it is not discussed more in the ADHD community, because Yoga Nidra can help reduce stress, anxiety, and insomnia. Just what our brains need, right?

You know that intense fatigue when you're too tired to think or do anything? When you've burnt all the oil that could be burnt, and it's not even mid-afternoon, and you still have a ton of things on your to-do list? Well, Yoga Nidra to the rescue!

At first glance, it can look like another form of guided meditation, but it goes way beyond that. You practice it by lying down, which takes you into a deep state of rest without falling asleep. It's an extraordinary sensation. It allows you to unwind and recharge simultaneously, both physically and mentally. It's like a power nap for body and mind.

Want to know the science behind it? I've got you! It can increase the activity in the prefrontal cortex. You know, that's the part of the brain responsible for decision-making, attention, and self-control. It can also decrease the activity in the amygdala. That's the part of the brain responsible for the fight-or-flight response. That was measured in a study on the impact of Yoga Nidra on the mental health of college professors.

So if you're feeling mentally or physically exhausted, or both, try it and thank me later. You'll find lots of guided yoga nidra relaxations out there, including in the apps Insight Timer and Down Dog mentioned earlier.

15. THERAPY

Ah, therapy. I guess I've been keeping the most obvious for last. You might not want to hear this, but therapy helps. Well, it often helps.

Of course, there are a lot of therapies you can choose from, but Cognitive Behavioral Therapy (CBT) and Dialectical Behavioral Therapy (DBT) are the ones that get raving reviews when it comes to managing ADHD.

CBT

Right, so what is it?

It's a form of talk therapy that focuses on identifying and changing negative thought patterns and behaviors.

Okay, great. So how can it help adults with ADHD?

> It focuses on negative thought patterns and behavior and creates new coping strategies to improve a particularly problematic behavior. So it usually revolves around practical daily functioning issues like time management, organization, focus, productivity, or self-esteem.

> Now, let's be real, does it actually work?

> Well, according to research, the answer is basically yes!

A meta-analysis of 19 studies published in the Journal of Consulting and Clinical Psychology found that CBT has a super positive effect on ADHD symptoms. And the best part? It was particularly effective for adults! It's so good, I'm going to mention one more study - there was a notable one published in the Journal of the American Academy of Child & Adolescent Psychiatry that found that CBT was just as effective as medication in reducing ADHD symptoms. I mean, wow! [Cue applause]

DBT

Okay, let's turn to DBT now. The new kid on the block! Well, it was developed in the 1970s but is less known than CBT. Originally, it was designed for people with personality disorders, but now it's being used for various issues, including ADHD and anxiety.

> So, what is that one?

> The acronym stands for Dialectical Behavioral Therapy, and it's a blend of CBT and mindfulness. You already know how both can help people with ADHD, so it sounds good, right?

> But how does it work?

It's taking the best of CBT to create change but uses mindfulness to promote acceptance too. So while reframing thought patterns and behavior, you also accept your difficult emotions or situations. It focuses on emotional regulation, coping skills, communication, and relationships.

And does it really, really work?

Well, again, in short, yes!

According to a study published in the *Journal of Consulting and Clinical Psychology*, DBT can effectively treat individuals with ADHD.

Therapy ain't cheap, but those types of behavioral psychotherapies are usually limited in time, and sometimes available in group settings, so you're not signing up for ten years of lying down on a couch. Depending on where you live, you might even be able to get some sessions as part of your treatment plan. It's certainly worth looking into it as we shouldn't underestimate the power of working with another human, whether it is one-on-one or as a group.

You are now armed with 15 proven techniques that can make a hell of a difference to your life. So put your best experimental mindset on, explore, give them a try, collect your findings, and stick with the ones that work best for you. In the next chapter, we will dive deep into the complicated world of emotions, and all the tools we've just mentioned here will make you stronger to ride that rollercoaster.

empowering intermission

Are you ready to spread the love for "Empowered Women with ADHD" and uplift others on their ADHD journeys? Leaving a review on Amazon is as easy as 1-2-3:

1. Visit the book's page on Amazon.
2. Scroll down to "Customer Reviews."
3. Click "Write a customer review."

Pour your heart out, as if talking to a friend. Share insights and favorite parts. Describe how you're feeling reading the book. Highlight its unique tone.

Feel free to get creative! Add a photo or video for a personal touch.

To leave a review, visit: mybook.to/empoweredADHDbook

Or scan the QR code for direct access.

Spark that warm, empowering feeling. Your authentic review can ignite inspiration, guiding others to the support they long for.

Thank you for being an essential part of this empowering movement.

CHAPTER FIVE

empowered feelings

WHY ARE YOUR EMOTIONS ALL OVER THE PLACE AND WHAT CAN YOU DO ABOUT IT?

DO you ever feel like your emotions are in charge and you're just in the passenger seat? You're not alone. There are many of us who share this same feeling. Struggling with emotions often goes hand in hand with ADHD, and the effects can be devastating. I don't mean to dampen the mood here. I just mean that the pain is real and the struggle can be serious.

There are many reasons for that, and the good news is that we've already covered some ground. With all those racing thoughts, an overwhelmed mind is a very fertile ground for intense emotions. So by calming the mind, as we saw in the previous chapter, you're already giving yourself a head start. Remember that the best thing you can do once you've found a technique you like is to practice it daily so it becomes second nature when you need it most.

Another thing that can trigger emotions is sensory overload. When your senses are bombarded with too much information, it can cause a meltdown. So revisit part 5 in Chapter 3 if you need it. That's the one on sensory problems. It's worth making the adjustments that work for you, as it could make a huge difference to your emotional well-being.

So now that you've got those tools under your belt, let's explore three main causes of dysregulated emotions when it comes to

ADHD. And, yes, of course, we'll also look at strategies to cope with them.

I. Emotional Dysregulation

Okay, if you're unfamiliar with the term, emotional dysregulation is when your emotions seem to have a mind of their own and go from zero to a hundred faster than a cheetah on skates. You might find yourself feeling super angry, anxious, or sad in no time flat. What's worse is that once you're there, controlling these emotions gets really tough.

Then not only is it a very uncomfortable place to be in, but it can also create mega problems in relationships, both at work and at home. People in your life, as well as complete strangers, might struggle to understand why you're reacting like that.

Emotional dysregulation in ADHD brains is like having a turbulent flight of emotions with no seatbelts.

What Does Science Say?

A study published in the *Journal of Attention Disorders* found that adults with ADHD reported significantly higher levels of emotional dysregulation than adults without ADHD.

Okay, but why are we like that? The prefrontal cortex, which is like the "control center" for our emotions, might not be as active in people with ADHD. So it's looking like the commands on that turbulent flight are not in full power.

But emotional dysregulation can also be a result of the stress and frustration that comes with ADHD. It's like trying to read, listen to a podcast, eat, drink, and crochet - all at the same time while the plane is flying through a storm. And remember, we have no seatbelts and we've just been asked to put the oxygen mask on. I mean, give us a break!

Over time, this chronic stress can make it even harder to regulate our emotions. It's like a never-ending cycle of emotional turmoil. When stress is constant, our brains simply can't cope. Not just ADHD brains, by the way. Remember that prefrontal cortex we've just mentioned? Well, it just can't keep up with the demands. The pilot is doing their best, but the commands are losing power, the lights are flashing, and the storm is intensifying...! I don't know about you, but I feel stressed just thinking about it.

As a result, our emotional responses become more intense and unpredictable. The smallest things can trigger a flood of emotions, like a tiny spark igniting a box of fireworks. Your frustration may skyrocket, patience may dwindle, and the ability to bounce back from setbacks may feel out of reach.

But wait, there's more! Chronic stress not only affects your emotional regulation but also fuels the very symptoms of ADHD. It's a double whammy. The brain fog thickens, attention wavers, and impulsivity takes center stage, further complicating your efforts to navigate the tumultuous sea of emotions. Luckily, tools from the previous chapter can help minimize stress.

THE EMOTIONAL RIPPLE EFFECTS

Hands up, if your emotions affect your behavior, then you regret it, and then you start to feel ashamed and guilty, which adds more stress and worry to the equation. Yeah, my hand is definitely up!

That's called a secondary emotion and that's how we end up with two issues rather than just one! You've got the original emotion to deal with, and now you're also grappling with the shame and guilt of your reaction. Maybe you've shouted at your kids, or your boss, and you feel terrible about it. But it's like trying to put out a fire with gasoline – certainly not the best approach.

Tools for self-compassion are useful in this situation. Remember Chapter 4? We can use self-compassion tools like the pat-on-the-back list, talking to a friend or using one of the breathing exercises to calm down.

So, if you feel like your emotions are all over the place, take a deep breath and remember that you're not alone. Put that oxygen mask and seatbelt on as we examine the strategies that will help very soon, promise. Just after part 2, actually.

2. REJECTION SENSITIVITY

Let's talk about rejection sensitivity, or Rejection Sensitivity Dysphoria (RSD). It's not an official symptom of ADHD or a medical diagnosis, but it's something most women with ADHD experience. A study published in the *Journal of Attention Disorders* in 2012 examined the relationship between ADHD, RSD, and emotional dysregulation in adults. Once again, it found that those with ADHD were more likely to experience symptoms of RSD, such as intense emotional reactions to rejection, heightened anxiety in social situations, and a strong desire for social approval.

With RSD, every sideways glance or innocent comment becomes a personal attack, sending your emotions into a whirlwind. It's like wearing a magnifying glass over your heart, amplifying every perceived slight.

REJECTION SENSITIVITY DYSPHORIA

RSD

" WHILE it's LIKELY to be a LIFELONG JOURNEY, there are THINGS that can be DONE... "

And, together with ADHD, they can create a nasty, vicious cycle: your ADHD traits may lead to forgetfulness, disorganization, or impulsive actions, which can result in mistakes or misunderstandings. And guess what? RSD jumps right into the mix, making you feel like a failure, amplifying any criticism or rejection, and triggering intense emotional reactions, which may lead to more forgetfulness and the lot.

Some common reactions to rejection or perceived rejection are:

- Outbursts when rejected, including physical like anger or tears
- Becoming quiet or moody
- Feeling like a failure
- Becoming embarrassed or self-conscious
- Negative self-talk

- Becoming a people-pleaser
- Difficulty forming and maintaining relationships

It can look different for everyone, but RSD is no joke, and the intensity of the pain can feel excruciating. But please have hope; while it's likely to be a lifelong journey, there are things that can be done, so keep reading because help is on its way.

3. YOUR 7-STEP GUIDE TO REGULATING EMOTIONS

The good news is that if you've read the previous chapter, you are already well-equipped to deal with emotions. But there are other steps you can take to help you regain control and feel more at peace. We're going to look at seven ways to help you manage emotional dysregulation in the context of ADHD.

1. Long-term techniques

As mentioned in Chapter 4, DBT, CBT, mindfulness, journaling, and self-compassion, all help with emotional regulation. I wish I could tell you it's a matter of going through a painless five-minute procedure, but it's not. It's a life-long journey, and consistency is key. And I know it's tricky when consistency is one of the things we struggle with. But if you practice one or more of these techniques regularly, your general emotional regulation will likely improve, and the frequency and intensity of the emotions will reduce.

But what can we do right now? When we're feeling completely overwhelmed by emotions. I'm glad you asked. Let's take a look.

2. Step back and cool down

When emotions are running high, hit the pause button as soon as possible. For me, this is the cornerstone to managing any intense situation. If I manage to remove myself from the situation and wait, I'm 99% likely to react in a way that I will feel okay about.

So unplug, mute that chat, don't check that email, excuse yourself from the conversation, whatever it takes. Then take a walk, find a quiet space, have a sensory break, or practice breathing exercises. And just let it cool down.

3. Identify the feeling

Emotions can be sneaky little things hiding in the nooks and crannies of your body. Play detective and locate where it's lurking physically. Is it a knot in your stomach or a lump in your throat? It will help you better understand what you're experiencing and get to step 4.

4. Name it to tame it

What is that feeling? Is it anger? What kind of anger? Is it rage? Is it frustration? Try to pinpoint exactly what you're feeling. Giving it a name helps you understand it better and can even reduce its intensity. It's like shining a light on a shadowy figure, revealing its true nature.

5. Write, write, write!

Grab a pen and paper, or go digital and jot down your emotions and triggers. Once the storm has passed and the plane has stabilized, take a moment to reflect on what happened. Ask yourself questions like what triggered my emotions? How did I react? What could I do differently next time? Remember curious accountability in Chapter 2? That's a time when it can come in handy. It can help you identify patterns and potential solutions for managing those pesky emotions in the future.

6. Separate yourself from the emotion

Remember, you are not your emotions. Try this affirmation: "This is one isolated moment, not my entire life." It's like a gentle reminder that emotions are just temporary visitors. They will leave, and you're the one in control of your emotional house.

7. Shake it off

Channel your inner Taylor Swift and shake off those emotions! Go for a run, punch the air, or dance like nobody's watching because, frankly, nobody should be watching. Once it's behind you, finish it off with physical activity. It will help release any repressed emotions and energy that might be left.

Hopefully, you'll feel more empowered to regulate your emotions with this 7-steps framework. But remember that the power is in the longer-term solutions we've discussed. It's a journey, but you're on it anyway, so you might as well choose the path that helps you steer your emotions in a positive direction.

4. Hormones, moods, and Women with ADHD

I guess it is not groundbreaking to say that hormones can greatly impact our moods, right? (Yes, I'm looking at you, PMS). Well, annoyingly, for women with ADHD, that impact can be even bigger. That's because we're more prone to hormonal fluctuations, which can lead to emotional dysregulation.

A study in the *Journal of Clinical Psychology* revealed that our premenstrual symptoms are more severe compared to women without ADHD. I'm talking about lovely things like mood swings, anxiety, depression, and irritability. And that study was unequivocal because the findings were the same even after controlling for other factors such as age, hormonal contraception, and previous psychiatric history.

What I find really irritating, besides premenstrual symptoms (PMS), is that despite the clear impact of hormones on women with ADHD, there is still a lack of research. Many studies on ADHD have focused primarily on male participants, which means we still have much to learn about how hormones impact women with ADHD.

The Rockstar Hormone

Research suggests that there might be a connection between estrogen and ADHD symptoms in women. If you don't know about estrogen, let me introduce you. This hormone is like the rockstar of our body; it regulates the menstrual cycle, supports reproductive health, and quite likes to run the physiological show.

"Estrogens are not only crucial in sexual maturation and reproduction but are also highly involved in a wide range of brain functions, such as cognition, memory, neurodevelopment, and neuroplasticity." states a 2021 article in the *International Journal of Molecular Sciences* that looked at the Role of Estrogen Receptors and Their Signaling across Psychiatric Disorders, including ADHD.

So it turns out estrogen might have a secret influence on those ADHD symptoms. It's like estrogen is joining the ADHD squad for an impromptu dance-off.

One intriguing aspect is how estrogen levels party during the menstrual cycle. They rise and fall, and it seems that some women with ADHD experience change in their symptoms during these stunning hormonal performances. And the result of their wild behavior is decreased focus, increased impulsivity, and attention difficulties during specific phases of the menstrual cycle.

But estrogen doesn't stop there. It's also a sneaky player in the brain's chemical orchestra, known as neurotransmitters. Think of neurotransmitters as the maestros of mood, attention, and impulse control. Estrogen might just stroll in, pull out its baton, and start conducting the neurotransmitters symphony. It's believed that estrogen can influence the activity of certain neurotransmitters like dopamine and serotonin, which have a starring role in ADHD. So, estrogen might be playing a part in increasing the volume of those ADHD symptoms.

And guess what? Estrogen loves to dabble in the executive functions department too. You know, those cognitive processes that are responsible for planning, decision-making, and self-regulation. Estrogen waves its wand, and suddenly executive functions are caught up in a whirlwind.

Now, I need to add a word of caution. There is still a lot of unknown in the relationship between estrogen and ADHD and research is very new, so, hopefully more will be coming soon.

Each woman's experience with ADHD and estrogen is unique, so not all ADHD warriors will necessarily have a front-row seat to the estrogen show. If you're a menstruating woman with ADHD and you notice a suspicious correlation between your menstrual cycle and changes in your ADHD symptoms, it might be worth becoming a symptom detective. Track those symptoms throughout your cycle, gather clues, and develop strategies that fit your individual needs.

A WOMAN'S LIFE

Our hormones change throughout our life from puberty to menopause and, for some of us, through pregnancies. So as they change, so does their impact on ADHD symptoms.

We've already looked at the menstrual cycle, but it's really worth paying attention to its impact on our emotions. Interestingly, a study published in the *Journal of Attention Disorders* found that women with ADHD reported greater difficulty with emotional regulation during the premenstrual phase of their menstrual cycle compared to the follicular phase.

Pregnancy and postpartum bring their own hormonal challenges, so thrown in with the ADHD mix, it can be, well... interesting. Some women with ADHD will struggle more during pregnancy. At the same time, some can actually see an improvement in executive functioning, impulsivity, and hyperactivity, thanks to the increased level of estrogen and progesterone. Postpartum can be more tricky to navigate with fluctuating hormones, and there are also all the extra non-hormonal challenges like sleep deprivation.

Then pregnancy also raises the question of medication and what to do about it during pregnancy. Obviously, that's a conversation to have with your doctor, but the change in medication will of course impact your symptoms.

And then menopause hits, and the drop in estrogen levels can hit hard! So hard that we've got a whole other sub-chapter about it.

But don't you worry! As we're going to see a bit later, there are plenty of non-medication solutions to help manage ADHD symptoms during these hormonal ups and downs.

THE CH-CH-CHANGE

Ah, the joys of menopause. Hot flashes, mood swings, and sleep disturbances. It's like going through puberty all over again, but this time with wrinkles and a mortgage. And for women with ADHD, it can be even more challenging. You're not going to like what follows, but we're going to go through it together.

Research, like the one published in the *Menopause* journal, indicates that women with ADHD may face distinct challenges during menopause. The hormonal changes of menopause and peri-menopause can affect brain functions. So that makes executive functions and regulating emotion even trickier than they normally are.

Mood swings may be heightened during menopause for women with ADHD too. Hormonal fluctuations can interact with the existing emotional dysregulation associated with ADHD. The result? The world's wildest emotional rollercoaster just got wilder!

One study published in the *Journal of Women's Health* found that women with ADHD who were going through menopause reported higher levels of cognitive and emotional symptoms compared to women with ADHD who were not going through menopause.

However, it's important to note that limited research specifically focuses on the interaction between ADHD and menopause, so further investigation is still needed. But regardless of the data, what is crucial is for you to pay attention to your symptoms and take note of changes. You are the expert at you and you might need to advocate for yourself. If you feel that menopause is taking your ADHD symptoms to another level, consult with healthcare professionals who ideally understand both ADHD and menopause.

YOUR GUIDE TO MANAGING HORMONES

Managing hormones and ADHD can feel like a juggling act, but fear not! This practical guide is here to help you navigate the challenges and find a harmonious balance. With these tips, you can take charge of your hormonal journey and optimize your ADHD management like a pro.

1. Get to know your cycle

Keep a calendar or use a tracking app like "Clue" to note your periods' start and end dates. Tracking your menstrual cycle will help you anticipate hormonal shifts and adjust your ADHD management strategies accordingly.

Pay attention to any changes in ADHD symptoms, mood swings, or energy levels in the days leading up to your period. Recognizing PMS symptoms can help you plan ahead and implement coping mechanisms.

2. Establish consistent routines

Hormonal fluctuations can disrupt sleep patterns, which can worsen ADHD symptoms. Establish a consistent sleep routine to ensure you get quality rest and recharge your brain. Need help? Head back to Chapter 3.

Set regular times for meals, medication, exercise, and other activities. I know it sounds boring, and that's not what you want to hear but creating a structured daily routine provides stability and helps mitigate the impact of hormonal fluctuations on your ADHD symptoms.

3. Therapy

As we've seen before, therapy can also be incredibly helpful in managing ADHD symptoms, with cognitive-behavioral therapy (CBT) being a particularly effective approach to both ADHD and menopause symptoms. And remember to utilize the tools we've already discussed, like mindfulness meditation and sensory regulation techniques.

4. Diet

Diet can play a big role in regulating mood and energy levels, so focusing on eating a healthy, balanced diet with plenty of whole foods and limited sugar and caffeine is important. To freshen up your mind, refer to Chapter 3!

You could consider supplements like ginseng, St. John's Wort, black cohosh, and Ginkgo but check with your doctor first.

5. Communicate with your healthcare provider

Share your hormonal experiences. Discuss any changes you notice in your ADHD symptoms during different phases of your menstrual cycle or during perimenopause with your healthcare provider. If they're not listening, change your provider. I know it can be easier said than done. Still, they should be able to consider hormonal fluctuation when looking at your treatment. It might be non-pharmaceutical adjustments, or it could be a change in medication, or adding hormonal treatment, or alternative treatments.

6. Prioritize self-care

I know planning a treat can still seem like too much work when you're exhausted and overwhelmed. But I will repeat it one more time: the highest form of self-care is not a bubble bath; it is looking after yourself. So back to the basics: eat well, sleep well, move well.

Once that's in place, give your brain a mini spa experience - remember meditation, breathing exercises, yoga nidra, etc? Revisit to find a relaxing practice you like.

Now we can look at relaxing treats, and if it's a bubble bath, you've got my blessing! It could also be a walk with a friend, a pottery class, or reading a good book.

7. Build a support network

Talk about it. Hormones, pregnancy, cycles, and particularly menopause are no longer the taboo subjects they used to be.

While you keep in mind that your journey is unique, comparing notes can be very helpful. You will likely find that you're not the only one with those symptoms, and finding someone who understands can be so comforting.

Feel free to talk to your partner, close friends, and family members, even if they're not going through the same thing. It will help them understand why you are feeling or behaving in a certain way.

It is undeniable that hormones impact our ADHD symptoms, and it is infuriating that there isn't more research to guide us on this journey. However, you've now learned how to play detective and advocate for yourself along the way when seeking help from health providers. And there are a lot of practical tools you can use to manage the hormonal dance, so give them a try. I haven't mentioned humor and patience, but they're probably worth a mention, too, as they can be precious allies on this path.

CHAPTER SIX

empowered at home

FROM A FRAZZLING HOUSE TO A CALMING HOME

DO you know that feeling of walking into a room and getting completely frazzled by the clutter and mess? As someone with ADHD, this feeling can be amplified, making it even harder to manage our surroundings and feel calm in our own space. It's like we're constantly bouncing between two modes: either we can't see the mess at all and let it pile on, or we get so overwhelmed by it that we don't even know where to start.

Let's be real; a messy house is just a way of life for some of us. And if it doesn't bother you, then there's no need to stress about it. Forget what Aunty Karen said - having a messy house doesn't make you a bad person, and naturally tidy people are not morally superior. The only reason I'm interested in sharing tips about tidying your house is that for many of us with ADHD, a messy home can be a real source of overwhelm and frustration.

As ADHD brains, we like to live life on our own terms and rules. But on the other hand, we need a bit of structure to keep things under control and to bring some calmness into our daily lives. That's where routines come in handy! Now, I know what you're thinking, "routines are boring and rigid." But trust me; they can actually be freeing and create space in your brain for more exciting things.

Believe it or not, the state of your home can greatly impact your mental health and well-being. A cluttered home can lead to feelings of stress and anxiety, while a clean and organized space can boost self-esteem and improve overall mood.

"But where do I start?" I hear you cry. Step this way, and I'll show you all the tricks and tips I learned the hard way.

1. SIMPLIFY

First things first: declutter your space. Sorry, I know it's not what you want to hear, but here is the simple truth: the less stuff you own, the less time you need to spend tidying up.

I know what you're thinking: "It's all very well, but it's easier said than done. *How* and *what* exactly should I declutter? I don't know where to start in this giant mess?"

Alright, let's talk about it then! I hear you. I know exactly how it feels when the clutter is screaming in your face. So, here are 11 steps to make decluttering less daunting and more achievable:

1. Find your why

Take a minute to ponder why you would like a clean and tidy home. Is it to feel less frazzled? Is it to be able to invite friends at the last minute? Keep it in mind, or even better, write it down in your journal.

2. Small start and maximize impact

Instead of trying to tackle the whole house at once, start with one area that's causing you the most stress and will give you the most satisfaction to see clutter-free. It'll give you a sense of accomplishment and motivation to keep going. If you're not sure where to start, floors and surfaces are usually a good start. Still not sure? Try one of those: kitchen countertop, dinner table, living room couch, coffee table, or bedroom floor.

3. Set a timer

Sometimes, working in short bursts of time can be helpful, and it's particularly true when we're stuck and feel completely overwhelmed by a giant mess. So pick one of those strategic areas mentioned above and set a timer for 10-15 minutes. Focus on decluttering for that time only. Once the timer's off, if you're in the mood and you've started to hyperfocus, surf the wave and keep at it.

4. Enroll a buddy (at home or remote)

Decluttering can be more fun (and less overwhelming) when you have someone to support you. Whether it's a friend, family member, or a virtual accountability partner, having someone cheer you on can make all the difference. If you live with other people, try to rope them in and do it all together at the same time, you can even turn it into a little competition.

5. Apply the 80/20 rule

We typically only use 20% of our stuff 80% of the time. Keep this in mind when deciding what to keep or donate.

6. Three boxes system

One to donate, one to throw, one to keep. This simple system can make decluttering easier. Label three boxes and sort items into them as you go. This will help you see progress and decide what to keep or let go. This is my spin on the traditional four boxes technique where there is also a 'decide later box.' But in the ADHD world, that could be a recipe for disaster, and we could end up with a 'decide later box' hanging around for months if not years. Talking of time...

7. Get rid of things quickly

Don't let those garbage and donate boxes sit around, or they'll become clutter themselves. Get rid of them as soon as possible. Yes, do consider the environment and an ethical way of disposing of them but don't agonize over it. Get them out of the house.

8. Give a home to things

If the things you want to keep don't already have a home, pick one. This will make it easier to put them away and keep them organized in the future.

9. Put things back immediately

Same reason as the objects you're getting rid of; you want to avoid a box of things to put back to stay there for months. So don't wait to fill the box or finish decluttering the whole room. Put things back after you've successfully tackled each surface or little area. If you're working with a timer, then make sure the last few minutes are dedicated to putting things back so you end the session on an empty box.

10. Buy less and say no to free stuff

Well, unless they really, really "spark joy!" We all know how tempting it is to take free stuff, but it's important to remember that clutter adds up fast. Be mindful of what you bring into your home and only keep what you truly need or love.

11. Repeat

Sorry, a decluttering job is never over. But... it gets A LOT easier after the first one. Don't forget that decluttering is an ongoing process, not a one-time event. Keep at it, and celebrate your progress along the way! You also want to banish perfectionism and accept that a bit of mess is often part of the ADHD diagnosis.

Remember, the sense of accomplishment and the peace of mind that comes with living in a clutter-free environment. Start somewhere, and you will soon experience a little dopamine boost every time you see a clear surface.

2. TACKLING THE FLOORDROBE

Here comes the infamous floordrobe - the perfect example of how ADHD can wreak havoc on our organizing skills.

It's like a magical transformation occurred overnight, turning your room into a runway of disarray. Shirts and pants become confetti, scattered haphazardly in a celebration of fashion freedom. Socks and underwear form rebellious alliances, daring you to find their rightful pairs. The floordrobe is a living, breathing entity, constantly evolving and expanding its boundaries.

The floordrobe (or chairdrobe) is such a vast topic that it deserves to be tackled separately. But as always, I've got you! With these three simple tools, you can tackle that pile of clothes and turn your room into a sanctuary of tidiness (or close enough).

Capsule Wardrobe

It's my ADHD fashionista's secret weapon against the mighty floordrobe! Picture this: a curated collection of stylish and functional clothing carefully chosen to minimize decision fatigue and maximize fashion flair.

But what exactly is a capsule wardrobe, you ask? Think of it as decluttering for your clothes. A capsule wardrobe is a simplified wardrobe with a maximum of 50 items that all go well together. Having one can save time and reduce the pile of clothes on your floor. Depending on where you live, you can have different capsule wardrobes for different seasons. Just imagine the dopamine boost of always looking stylish and only wearing items you love.

The beauty of the capsule wardrobe lies in its simplicity. Instead of drowning in a sea of clothes, you carefully select a limited number of versatile pieces you truly love and feel fabulous in. This not only saves precious time and energy but it also helps you stay focused and organized amidst the chaos of ADHD.

To create your very own capsule wardrobe, start by sorting through your current clothing collection and bid farewell to those pieces that no longer spark joy or fit your personal style. The floordrobe's reign ends here!

Then select a few versatile, high-quality items that form the foundation of your capsule wardrobe. Keep in mind what you spend your time doing. Do you work in an office and wear suits all the time? Do you live in tracksuits? Put those center stage and pick additional pieces for those other occasions.

Now, let's take another look at that floor. Is it clear yet?

No Half Measures

When it comes to the clothes on your floor, it's either dirty or clean. That gray zone of "I've worn it once, so it's not clean, but I could wear it again" is the main culprit for the floordrobe.

If they're clean enough to wear again, they're clean enough to go back into your wardrobe. If it grosses you out and you don't consider them clean enough to return to your closet, they belong in the laundry basket. Whichever it is, don't let them linger on the floor for days.

If you're comfortable putting them back in your wardrobe, but you're worried they will never get washed, you can simply put them back the wrong way around so you know their days are numbered. Or, if you want to be extra organized, buy cloth hangers of a different color for those half-dirty items.

Simplifying Laundry

Laundry, oh laundry, it never seems to end and is a huge factor in clothes-related headaches, too. But with these simple hacks, you'll be able to simplify your laundry routine and maybe even have a little fun doing it:

I know the queen of decluttering, Mari Kondo, has taught us how to fold everything so it wouldn't take space in the drawers, but let's rebel: folding is not for everyone! And you don't need to fold every single piece of underwear for the whole family if it makes you die inside. Like it's equally boring twin ironing, folding doesn't make you morally superior. If it's not your thing, don't worry about it, and let's look at three tricks that keep folding to a minimum.

1. Hang it up

Give your wallet and the planet a break: skip the dryer! Reduce folding time by putting clothes on hangers to dry. Then they can go straight back into the wardrobe. That's when you can start feeling pretty smug about having limited clothes (50 items or less) and therefore space in your closet.

And this technique comes with an added benefit! It will minimize your need for ironing too. Most fabric drying on hangers will be fine to wear as they are or can be ironed in no time.

2. Banish pairs

Shall we talk about the nightmare of pairing socks? And if you're doing laundry for a family of four in the winter, we're talking about 56 socks that need pairing weekly! Yes, I've done the math, and I hope you can feel my pain.

The best hack is to get each person a batch of the exact same socks so you don't have to waste time matching them up. You don't even need to fold them! Just open your drawer and grab two!

3. Just do it

Okay, sometimes some items need to be folded. In this case, do it immediately as you take the laundry out of the dryer or off the peg and return them to their designated place. This saves time, and you don't live fishing out clean items from the laundry basket. Yeah, I've done it for years.

3. MAINTAINING, AKA TIDYING + CLEANING

Let's get this straight: tidying up with ADHD is a whole new adventure. But once we have gone through a wild and whimsical journey through the land of scattered socks, mysterious dust bunnies, and misplaced treasures, we want to keep the peaceful feeling that comes from a clutter-free home for as long as possible.

ADHD and cleaning go together like a squirrel and a shiny acorn, but not to worry, for in this wacky adventure, we shall uncover the secrets to taming the chaos and keeping order in your space.

ADHD and Tidying Up

Let's embrace the unique challenges (and their solutions) that ADHD brings to the cleaning party. Our minds may wander like curious butterflies, flitting from one task to another, but that's okay! We thrive on excitement and spontaneity, turning mundane chores into captivating quests. So, put on your imaginary superhero cape because it's time to conquer the mess with these 6 tips!

1. The Polished Pockets

Now, there's a little controversy in the ADHD community around paying someone to do your dirty laundry. Literally. Or any other house-cleaning chores, for that matter. A lot of women feel shame and guilt around that. Let's talk straight: your worth as an individual, even as a wife or a mother, is not measured by your ability to keep house. We're not in Victorian times anymore.

You are worthy, you have many talents, and if cleaning is not one of them and you have the means then by all means hire a cleaner. No shame in that game! This is self-care and a better investment than a spa day if you ask me. You're worth it. And if you can't afford it, you're not alone, and all is not doomed - keep reading: the chores of today are self-care acts you're paying forward.

2. The Distractibility Dance

As we clean, our attention might jump from dusting a shelf to examining an old photo album or discovering a forgotten toy.

Shift your mindset and embrace the dance by turning cleaning into a scavenger hunt—seek out hidden treasures while still making progress. Who knows what fascinating artifacts you'll find along the way?

3. The Time-Warp Whirlwind

Time has a naughty habit of slipping through our fingers like slippery soap. But fear not, brave soul!

Plan a regular cleaning time, whether it's a weekend morning or a few minutes every day. Consistency is key when it comes to maintaining a tidy space. Set aside dedicated time for cleaning and make it a habit.

You can also set timers or alarms to keep you on track, turning cleaning into a race against the clock. Can you finish tidying before the buzzer sounds? Embrace the challenge, and let time be your ally, not your foe.

4. The Clutter Carousel

Ah, the Clutter Carousel, where things seem to spin in never-ending circles.

To conquer this merry-go-round of mess, break tasks into bite-sized chunks. Clean one corner of a room at a time, or tackle a specific category, like clothes or books. With each completed job, you'll feel the satisfaction of stepping off the carousel and into a clutter-free zone. You could also create a task list, so you know what needs to be done and can check off each item as you go.

Remember those focus areas you wanted to declutter first? Keep focusing on them. Your study might be a mess, but as long as your kitchen and living room are tidy, you have a place to rest and invite friends.

5. The Motivation Mixer

Motivation is that elusive ingredient we sometimes struggle to find. Fear not, for you hold the power to mix up a motivational concoction of your own.

Crank up your favorite tunes, dance with the vacuum cleaner, and envision the joy of a clean and organized space. Not a fan of broomstick dancing? Put on your favorite podcast or audiobook, let your imagination run wild, and transform cleaning into some well-deserved intellectual 'me time.'

6. The Expedient Exercise

Are you a fan of killing two birds with one stone? I am. As you know, I'm not a fan of exercise for exercise's sake. But I know that movement and a tidy space both help my mental health, so I like to combine them! Boom!

A bit of music is good for motivation but can also give you a little spring in your walk. And if that's not enough, wear ankle or wrist weights or both. Squat to reach the laundry basket or plates in the dishwasher. Or run up and down the stairs when you need to put things back! Turn your house into a gym and chores into the latest workout.

7. The Reward Rendezvous

Cleaning can be a thankless task, but not on our watch!

Set up a reward system to celebrate your triumphs along the way. Treat yourself to a delicious snack, take a break to watch a funny cat video, or maybe it's time to indulge in that bubble bath. Let the rewards fuel your enthusiasm and keep the cleaning fun alive! Or plan to have a friend over once you're done for extra motivation!

Remember, tidying up is a journey, and embracing your quirks along the way is perfectly okay. Find what works best for you, celebrate your progress, and don't forget to reward yourself for a job well done.

Cooking

Ah, cooking! One of life's necessary evils. A dance of flavors, a symphony of ingredients, and a delightful playground for the ADHD brain. However, amidst the excitement and culinary creativity, unique challenges come with cooking when you have ADHD.

Whether you're a family chef or a solo cook, you might find yourself wandering around the kitchen, searching for that elusive spice or that key ingredient you swear you had just a moment ago. Every time you cook, it's like a treasure hunt with unexpected surprises and occasional victories. Remembering to preheat the oven, set timers, and keep track of cooking durations can feel like a whirl-wind for the ADHD chef.

But for me, it is just another thing to think about and organize when there are other things I'd rather do and a million other things in my head. But we also know that eating well is important for managing symptoms, so here are five useful strategies to make the experience less overwhelming.

1. Meal planning

The magic of meal planning lies in its ability to provide clear directions and alleviate decision fatigue while saving time and energy. Now, I can see my younger self rolling her eyes and thinking, "What have I become?" But my younger self is not trying to keep a family of four healthy while juggling tons of other responsibilities.

So, don't listen to her and listen to me instead.

Sit down with a pen and paper (or your favorite digital tool) and brainstorm meal ideas for the week. Consider your dietary preferences, available ingredients, and the level of effort you're willing to put into each meal. From there, create a schedule of what you'll cook each day, taking into account any time constraints or special occasions.

But wait, there's more! If you keep those plans for a few weeks, you can soon put them on a rotation and never have to think about what's for dinner ever again.

2. Weekly grocery shopping

Meal planning also brings the gift of efficiency. By jotting down your grocery list based on your planned meals, you can navigate the supermarket with purpose and avoid those aimless wanderings down the snack aisle (let's be honest, sometimes those are necessary too).

It saves you from the chaos of missing ingredients and impulsive trips to the store. By planning and stocking up once a week, you ensure that your kitchen is well-prepared for your culinary endeavors and you can free that part of your brain.

Extra tip: if supermarket deliveries are an option for you, they are worth looking into. Some have features allowing you to save lists, freeing even more headspace. Not to mention that supermarkets can be particularly taxing if you're subject to sensory overload.

3. Batch cook

You need to cook healthy meals, so you might as well make it worth your while. Cook in bulk, portion out, and freeze what you don't need. Easy. It will save you time and energy later on. Now, here's the real magic: when hunger strikes or you're too exhausted to cook, you simply reach into your stash, and voila! A delicious, homemade, healthy, and ADHD-friendly meal is ready to be enjoyed.

That's another self-care act you're paying forward.

4. Prep

No, I'm not talking about surviving in the wilderness. By prepping your ingredients ahead of time, you'll have your veggies sliced, proteins marinated, and whole food cooked like a culinary ninja. When it's meal time, you can assemble healthy, nutritious meals in minutes. Make prepping food part of your weekend routine.

You think it's boring? That's another mindless task you can do while listening to a podcast or chatting on the phone. You can even turn it into a workout.

5. Subscribe

If you have the means or can ask for help, why not consider a healthy food subscription service? They deliver pre-made meals or meal kits with all the ingredients straight to your door, taking the planning hassle out of cooking.

Make It Stick

The best way to stick to something is to fit it into a routine. Enters habit stacking. It's a bit like playing Jenga with your habits - you stack them on top of each other and hope they don't come tumbling down.

Basically, it's about building new habits by attaching them to existing ones. For instance, I keep my room floordrobe clutter-free by putting my clean enough clothes back in the wardrobe while I get dressed the following day. This works for me because I always get dressed at some point in the day, and that's when my brain is happy to think about clothes.

Interested? Here is how it's done:

1. Identify a current habit

Find a routine you already do consistently and use it as a trigger for your new habit. Think about the most basic ones, like "I get out of bed."

2. Start small

Don't try to take on too much at once. Start with a small habit and build from there. Think super easy. It should be a task that you can do in less than 2 minutes. For instance, "When I finish eating dinner, I will put my plate into the dishwasher." Notice how I didn't pick "once I've finished dinner, I will clean the kitchen." That would be too big and too vague to make it stick.

3. Be consistent

Consistency is key when building a new habit, which makes it tricky for us. That's why it is best to pick a fundamental habit that you do every day. It takes time to build a practice, so be patient with yourself.

4. Track it down

Habit tracking might help you stick to it and help you remember to do it. It's definitely beneficial when it is a brand-new habit.

You can go analog in your journal or use one of the many habit tracker apps out there. I use TickTick for that too, but you could also look into Habitica if you want to gamify it a little.

5. Find what works for you

As with anything in life, there is no one-size-fits-all approach to habit stacking. Experiment with different triggers and habits to find what works best for you. Remember your experimental mindset. If it doesn't want to stick, don't give up. Try a different trigger, break it down even more, or see how you could make it even easier to perform.

I know that advice on tidying up can be almost as overwhelming as the mess itself. So remember to go gently and focus on the long haul. Start small, build from there, and you'll be fine.

CHAPTER SEVEN

empowered at work

HOW TO TACKLE IMPOSTOR SYNDROME, IMPULSIVITY, AND PROCRASTINATION WHILE USING YOUR STRENGTHS TO THRIVE AT WORK

AH, the joys of adulting and work life! Are you tired of feeling like your brain is working against you in the workplace? Do you feel like you're constantly struggling to keep up with your peers or failing to live up to your potential? Well, fear not, my friend, because, in this chapter, we will explore how to become empowered at work! That's right. We're going to tackle the three main challenges women with ADHD face in their careers and show you how to use your unique strengths to your advantage.

Get ready to learn how to overcome obstacles, thrive in your job, and finally unleash your full potential at work. So buckle up and get ready to try some awesome tools and hacks to help you become the boss lady you were always meant to be!

1. MINDSET (AGAIN)

Did you think we've covered all there is to know about mindset in Chapter 2? Think again. Mindset work is never done, and I'd like to reframe our mindset specifically with work in mind. I see too many ADHD women who feel held back by ADHD when it comes to their career achievements or simply think their impairments are too big to be able to do anything fulfilling workwise. It really doesn't have to be that way, so let's tackle this right now!

Tackle Imposter Syndrome

Impostor syndrome is the sneaky little voice in our head that tells us we're not good enough, smart enough, or qualified enough for our job. And for women with ADHD, that voice can be even louder and more persistent. Many adults and children with ADHD have trouble accepting positive feedback about themselves.

But let's back up a bit. What exactly is impostor syndrome? Well, it's the feeling of inadequacy or self-doubt despite evidence of success or competence. People with impostor syndrome often feel like a fraud and fear being exposed as such.

While impostor syndrome can certainly hold you back in your career, as we will see, it's also possible to use your ADHD to your advantage. Research even shows that when people with ADHD feel supported and valued at work, they can thrive and make significant contributions.

So how can you tackle impostor syndrome?

First and foremost, look after your mental well-being. Revisit and use the strategies laid out in Chapter 4 for some tips and tools on how to manage ADHD-related stress and anxiety.

Okay, I hear you. What else can you do when it hits in the middle of a workday? Here are five steps you can take to gracefully swat away that imposter like a pesky mosquito:

1. Recognize the feeling

Talk about it with someone. It can be your therapist, it can be a fellow ADHD woman, or a friend; just naming it will help.

2. Check the facts

Look for evidence, and write it down: was it really that bad? What are your wins?

3. Rephrase your thoughts

If you really screwed up, then use the power of "yet" or "how can I." Remember curious accountability and growth mindset from Chapter 4?

4. Reframe competition

If a colleague is good at something, learn from it rather than indulge in envy.

5. Celebrate

Acknowledge what you've done well. Do it regularly, do it often. Depending on what your work is, it could be after each major project or a monthly occurrence.

PLAY TO YOUR STRENGTHS

There are jobs that are better suited to women with ADHD, so we might as well play to our strengths. First of all, it's important to recognize what those strengths are. If you don't have a whole list that springs to mind, go and revisit Chapter 2. Now, according to the experts, people with ADHD tend to excel in jobs that involve creativity, variety, high intensity, and movement.

But let's get down to business. What are some of the best jobs for women with ADHD? Well, there are plenty of options, but here are a few career paths that are particularly well-suited to our unique set of skills.

Creative fields

This is where we can let our creative side shine! This includes jobs like graphic design, copywriting, or photography. These are great if you have good attention to detail and the ability to work on multiple projects. Also, anything in film or theater, where intensity can get pretty high.

Emergency responders

If you thrive in high-pressure situations and can make quick decisions under stress, careers like EMT, emergency room doctor or nurse, paramedic, or firefighter might be right up your alley.

Sales

If you're a natural talker, like thinking on your feet, and love the rush of closing a deal, a career in sales might be perfect for you.

Hospitality

From a chef, which requires creativity, attention to detail, and the ability to work in a fast-paced environment, to a bartender for bubbly folks who enjoy meeting different people and being on their feet, the possibilities are endless. Or, if you prefer to freelance, you could look at event planning or catering.

Entrepreneurship

Many people with ADHD are natural risk-takers and love the thrill of starting something new. Starting your own business might be the ultimate way to play to your strengths. You've got the added benefits of setting things up on your terms and creating the adjustments you need with a company culture of care.

15 Minutes of Fame

Who says being neurodivergent means you can't achieve greatness? ADHD affects people from all walks of life, including some of history's most successful and influential individuals. It's no wonder, given all those great qualities to celebrate about ADHD.

From artists and musicians to entrepreneurs and athletes, many famous people have openly shared their experiences with ADHD. So if you need any extra inspiration, here is a (very) short list of people with ADHD who have done very well for themselves:

- Richard Branson
- Jamie Oliver
- Bill Gates
- Zooey Deschanel
- Liv Tyler

- Solange Knowles
- Lisa Ling
- Michelle Rodrigez
- Mel B
- Simone Biles
- Emma Watson

This only includes the people who have been outspoken about it. If we start to delve into the dead ones who we now suspect had ADHD, oh boy! Does Wolfgang Amadeus Mozart, Leonardo Da Vinci, and Albert Einstein sound familiar to you?

2. Productivity

For women with ADHD, things can get a little tricky when it comes to organization, punctuality, and memory. These are the obvious ones, but annoyingly, these are often required at work. So keeping track of tasks, deadlines, and meetings can feel like juggling flaming swords while riding a unicycle.

Don't fret, though! I have so many awesome tricks for you up my sleeve.

7 Steps to Plan and Schedule Like a Pro

1. Set up goals

What do you want to be done? What's the end result? When does it need to be done? Write it down.

2. Break. It. Down

Now, big goals can be overwhelming, so break them down into smaller, more manageable tasks. For example, for me, 'write a book' becomes 'write an outline.' Then, I break that down even further into specific tasks like fact-checking references for a particular chapter. If you're really struggling with this, goblin.tools could be of great help. It's a free AI website that breaks down tasks for you.

3. Schedule

Give each task a designated time slot and write it in your diary. Goblin.tools can also help you estimate how long each task will take.

4. Organize

Organize your tasks based on their importance or their type. For instance, if some jobs involve buying things, group all the "buying jobs" so you can handle them in one go.

5. Prioritize

When planning your day, only select three must-do. Put the less urgent things in a nice-to-do tasks list, and leave everything else on a larger to-do list to pick from later. You can use many different tools for this, like the daily planner I've made for you, a bullet journal, or an app like TickTick (which is my favorite) or Notions.

6. Plan

Spend a few minutes at the end of each day to plan for the next day and at the end of the week to plan for the next week. It serves two purposes: First, it prevents procrastination the next day, as you will know exactly where to start. Second, it calms the mind for the rest of the day or the weekend, as your brain is not constantly planning in the background. It's like closing the work tabs on your browser so you can enjoy the leisure and rest tabs.

7. One task at a time

Multitasking may seem like a good idea, but it can actually hinder productivity. So, single-task your way to success! Avoid multitasking by blocking out time for each individual task.

Scheduling and planning isn't a habit one can learn and perfect overnight, but they can quickly create major improvements. So, give yourself the time and space to do it. But planning and scheduling can't do miracles if we don't eliminate distractions, so let's talk about that.

5 Tools to Banish Distractions

We all know how easy it is to get sidetracked by our phones, social media, a noise in the background, what should I cook for dinner, let's check Pinterest for new high-protein recipes, oh, that's a pretty pillow. Oh, wait... What was I doing? You can relate, right?

But here are my go-to techniques that help me stay in the work zone for a bit longer. Give them a go.

1. Give your phone the cold shoulder

Turn off your phone while you work. Or if it's too hardcore, put it in a drawer. Or if you need to stay on call, use a special app that turns off certain apps.

2. Cancel that noise

Earplugs, ear defenders, or headphones can block out background noises that might distract you from your work. And if you're not a fan of complete silence, try listening to white noise. There are tons of free apps and playlists.

3. Focus with music

Some tracks are specifically designed to help with focus. I use a free app called Endel, which creates personalized soundscapes. And there are plenty of playlists out there that are tailored to people with ADHD.

4. Pomodoro technique

It's basically putting a timer on. Now, I know it sounds a bit silly, but bear with me. The idea is simple - you work in focused bursts for a set amount of time and then take a short break. Personally, I like to surf the hyperfocus flow for 50 minutes when I'm in the zone. Then I switch to 25 minutes when procrastination hits. You can obviously use your phone timer or an app.

TickTick, my favorite app ever, has a Pomodoro mode. Flora and Forest are other cool options because they also stop you from checking other apps.

5. Body doubling

It's not a dance partner (although that would be fun); it's more of a productivity buddy. Now I must admit, I use this technique more for tackling home chores than work, but some people absolutely love it for work tasks. You can rope in a buddy or a colleague, or if you prefer a virtual twist, apps and websites like Focusmate, Flowclub, and Caveday can connect you with others who are also looking for some accountability. And guess what? There are even Facebook groups dedicated to this kind of stuff.

So whether you're rocking the Pomodoro Technique or finding a body double, there are plenty of effective ways to boost your productivity and conquer these tasks. Happy ticking, doubling, and getting stuff done!

3. WORKING WITH PEOPLE

Ah, people... [cue eye-roll.] If you have ADHD, you might find yourself struggling with some social situations in the workplace.

HOW TO MANAGE IMPULSIVITY

Do you know that urge to blurt out whatever is on your mind? Yep, that can definitely cause some social awkwardness. And do you find yourself jumping into conversations before others have finished speaking? It can be tough to wait, especially if you're excited or passionate about a topic.

It might be hard to stop and think before speaking, but it's worth a try. Some colleagues will love you for it if you acknowledge it and treat it with humor. But taking a deep breath and listening to others can also help build better relationships.

My absolute go-to trick is to write down the thought as it pops into my head. The main trigger for interrupting is the fear that we're going to forget, so if it is on paper, we can wave that fear goodbye and make that point when it's the right time.

Okay, sometimes, despite our efforts, conflict might arise. And let's face it, that's just part of working with other people, and it might have nothing to do with your ADHD. However, how we deal with it might be affected by it. So let's talk about handling conflicts and difficult conversations like a pro!

Remember Rejection Sensitive Dysphoria (RSD) from Chapter 4? The one that can make us feel extra sensitive to criticism or perceived rejection. Paired with impostor syndrome, it can lead to very dark places at work. It's important to remember that not everyone will agree with or like you, and that's okay. And in case of conflict, following these 7 steps should help:

1. Step back

First things first, if you're feeling overwhelmed or triggered, try taking a step back. It's okay to take a break, collect your thoughts, and take some deep breaths. Remember those breathing and reframing exercises from earlier chapters? They come in handy right about now.

2. Prepare

Next, prepare for the conversation by writing down your thoughts and key points.

Use simple and direct language and avoid getting defensive or blaming the other person. Instead, try using "I" statements to express how you feel without placing blame. For example, "I feel frustrated when..." instead of "You always do this..."

Remember, we're not trying to start (or win) a fight here; we're trying to resolve a conflict. So keep it cool, baby; be the bigger person.

3. Become solution-focused

Brainstorm solutions that work for both parties. Think outside the box and try to find creative solutions that meet everyone's needs.

4. Schedule

Choose a good time and place to have the conversation. You don't want to discuss sensitive issues in a noisy, crowded area where you're likely to be interrupted or distracted.

5. Listen

I know it can be an issue for us but listen actively and try to understand the other person's point of view.

Resist the urge to interrupt or argue, and take notes if necessary to remember your thoughts and responses.

5. Set boundaries

Boundaries are necessary to protect your mental health and well-being. Taking care of yourself and communicating your needs to others is important.

6. Reach out

If things are getting too heated, involving a manager or HR representative to mediate the conflict can be helpful.

TO DISCLOSE OR NOT TO DISCLOSE?

Ah, the dilemma of whether or not to disclose your ADHD at work. It can feel like you're standing at a crossroads while trying to navigate through a thorny forest of pros and cons. On the one hand, you may yearn for understanding, accommodations, and support. On the other hand, you worry about potential stigma, misconceptions, and the fear of being treated differently. It's a tough decision indeed.

When pondering this dilemma, consider a few key factors. First, think about the nature of your job. Are there specific challenges or tasks where accommodations could significantly enhance your performance? If so, disclosing your ADHD might open the door to reasonable adjustments that could level the playing field.

Next, evaluate the workplace culture. Is it inclusive, supportive, and understanding? Do you have colleagues or superiors who are open-minded and empathetic? If the environment fosters acceptance and diversity, disclosing your ADHD might be met with understanding and compassion.

However, it's also important to be aware of potential risks. Unfortunately, not all workplaces are accommodating or knowledgeable about ADHD. There may be misconceptions or biases that could affect how you are perceived or treated. In such cases, you might choose to keep your ADHD private and instead focus on self-management strategies that allow you to thrive without external accommodations.

You can also state your need for adjustments in a friendly way without mentioning neurodiversity. For instance, you can wear ear defenders to concentrate if you work in a noisy environment and tell your colleagues, "It helps me focus; nothing personal, folks." Or insist on taking your lunch break, saying, "I'm much more efficient after taking a break."

Once you have checked whether it is a legal requirement in your country, the decision to disclose or not is personal. It's about weighing the benefits against the risks and deciding what feels right for you. Trust your instincts, gather information about your rights and protections, and consider seeking advice from trusted professionals or support networks who can offer guidance based on their experiences.

4. The Long Haul

Managing work and ADHD temporarily can be easy and effective. Still, long-term fixes are what will truly make a difference. And the good news is there is plenty you *can* do to manage your ADHD (and, in fact, use it to your advantage) at work!

Use Your Hyperfocus Power

Now, let's dive into the magical realm of hyperfocus. Ah, the power of getting lost in the zone! When inspiration strikes and work feels effortless, embrace that hyperfocus like a boss. Ride that wave and knock out those tasks with superhero speed.

But, and this is a big BUT, make sure you take breaks during the workday to recharge those superpowers. Trust me; you'll come back even more performant than ever. When you feel like your brain needs a breather, take a break! Stretch those legs, do a little dance, or simply sit back and relax.

And breaks are not just during individual projects or between them —if you're employed, take some well-deserved paid time off. We often feel the need to overcompensate for any notion that we're not hardworking enough, but let me tell you, it's a surefire way to

Burn-Out City. So schedule breaks as well as tasks. A fresh mind will do better than one run down and exhausted!

SAY NO

Now, let's talk about the art of saying "no." It's a skill worth mastering. Don't overcommit yourself and spread yourself too thin, like vegan butter on toast. Know your priorities and take the time to think before committing to a new task, project, or job. And hey, don't be afraid to chat with someone about it—a partner, a friend, or even a trusted colleague. Sometimes a fresh perspective can help you make those tough decisions and keep your sanity intact.

Remember, my fellow ADHDers, managing ADHD at work in the long haul is all about finding the right balance between pushing your performance and taking care of yourself. So, conquer those tasks, take breaks like a pro, embrace your hyperfocus superpowers, and don't be afraid to say "no" when necessary.

ACCOUNTABILITY PARTNER

It's time to bring in the trusty sidekick, the accountability partner, to join us on our ADHD adventures in the workplace.

So, what exactly is an ADHD accountability buddy, you ask? Well, they're like the Chewbacca to your Han Solo or the peanut butter to your jelly (if you're into that kind of combo). They're here to support you, cheer you on, and keep you accountable to your goals. Whether it's a friend, a colleague, or even a fellow ADHD warrior, having someone in your corner can make all the difference.

CELEBRATE

Now, imagine this: you've conquered a challenging task, completed a project, or simply survived a particularly hectic day or week at work. You deserve a celebration! That's where your accountability partner can come in handy. They can shower you with virtual confetti. But don't rely solely on them for those pats on the back. Make it part of your own routine too!

Remember the pats on the back, the treats, and all that way back in Chapter 4? Use them at work! When you review your day and plan tomorrow, celebrate those wins, big or small, and acknowledge the superhero within you.

Going to work in a neurotypical office when you have ADHD is no easy feat. Remember to take it easy on yourself and have fun along the way. Choose the most fitting path to your abilities, and use that hyperfocus mode and streak of perfectionism to your advantage. Just remember where the pause button is and mind the burnouts, too!

CHAPTER EIGHT

empowered money

HOW TO CURB IMPULSIVE SPENDING, MANAGE DEBT, AND MAKE BUDGETING (ALMOST) FUN

WELL, well, well, let's dive into the exciting world of ADHD and finances. Just like the rollercoaster ride we've been on, managing money with ADHD can also be a thrilling adventure full of twists, turns, and the occasional loop-de-loop. While it may bring some extra challenges, fear not, friend, for there are strategies and tricks to help navigate the financial maze.

I. MONEY AND ADHD

Let's first acknowledge the impact of ADHD on our financial management. It's like having a squirrel in a room full of shiny objects. Our minds tend to wander, and our attention can easily be captured by that irresistible sale or the latest gadget that promises to solve all our problems (yes, I'm looking at you, neurodivergent-friendly earplugs I'm getting ads for on social media).

What about budgeting? And tracking expenses? That can feel like trying to tame a wild unicorn! Well, that can be as elusive as finding a mermaid in a sea of receipts. In all seriousness, though, ADHD can cost us a pretty penny. Here are only a few of the ways in which ADHD can become a real pain in our wallets' butt!

- **Impulsive spending** makes it challenging to stick to a budget or financial plan.
- **Emotional spending**: you know, that's when we use shopping as a way to cope with stress or seek temporary mood elevation (hello, dopamine boost).
- **Procrastination with financial tasks**, such as paying bills or organizing paperwork, can lead to missed deadlines and late fees.
- **Disorganization**: trouble organizing financial documents can make it challenging to track expenses and maintain a clear financial overview.
- **Forgetfulness**: when it comes to bill payment, due dates, and financial obligations, leading to potential financial consequences.
- **Difficulty with long-term planning**: ADHD can make it challenging to create and stick to long-term financial goals, such as saving for retirement or managing investments effectively.
- **Inconsistent budgeting** makes tracking income, expenses, and savings difficult.

I know it sounds bleak when you see it all as a list like that. But, as always, I've got you covered with some fixes and tricks. Let's take a look at them!

2. How to Manage Impulsive Spending

Come on now; we've all done it. That really expensive dress we thought was cute and bought on a whim? Or a pair of headphones we heard people rave about on TikTok? Hell! It could even be those new Stanley cups that have been breaking the bank. And if it is too much of a recurring problem, it can lead to serious issues. But as always, there are things you can do! Check these 8 techniques that can help.

1. Pause and ponder

Before making a purchase, take a moment to pause and ask yourself if it's a necessity or just a fleeting desire. Give your impulsive brain a chance to reconsider.

2. Window-shopping therapy

Instead of immediately hitting the "buy now" button, indulge in some virtual window shopping. Add items to your wishlist or save them for later. It satisfies the urge to shop without breaking the bank.

3. The 24-hour rule

Implement a self-imposed waiting period before making any significant purchases. Sleep on it, and if you still want it the next day, go for it. This helps filter out impulsive buys from genuine needs.

4. Budget buddies

Enlist a trusted friend or family member as your budget buddy. Before making a spontaneous purchase, consult with them. They can provide an objective perspective and help you stay on track.

5. Money mindfulness

Practice mindfulness techniques when it comes to your finances. Take a deep breath, reflect on your financial goals, and ask yourself if this purchase aligns with your priorities.

6. The distraction technique

Distract yourself from impulsive spending by engaging in other activities. Call a friend, take a walk, or work on a hobby. Redirecting your attention can help curb impulsive urges.

7. Cash-only challenge

Leave the credit card at home and switch to a cash-only system for a designated period. Having physical money in hand can make spending feel more tangible and help you stay within budget. Plus, it will keep the bigger purchases out of impulsive reach.

8. Reward-based budgeting

Set small financial goals and reward yourself when you achieve them. This helps create a positive association with responsible spending and motivates you to stay on track.

Like all the other tools I have shared with you so far, see which one works best for you, use it and abuse it. But getting impulsive spending under control might not be enough to bring balance to your financial situation or how you feel about it. So let's do a bit of mild adulting and delve into financial goals.

3. THREE FUN STEPS TO FINANCIAL GOALS

Setting financial goals is a journey that can be both exciting and challenging, especially when you have a touch of ADHD. And if you think it's boring, follow those three steps and reconsider.

1. Dream

You're the captain of your financial ship, charting a course toward your dreams. Embrace your imagination and visualize your goals in vibrant detail. Imagine your dream vacation, a cozy home, or that shiny new gadget you've been eyeing. Let your imagination run wild as you set sail on this financial voyage.

2. Consolidate

Now turn those ideas into a vision board or a "financial dreamland" collage. Cut out images from magazines or print them from the internet—whatever tickles your fancy. This visual representation will remind you of the amazing things you're working towards.

I would highly recommend going analog with glue sticks and scissors for this. It will help slow down your mind and make those associations in your brain. Plus, it will remove the temptation to click on a "buy now" link on Pinterest. But if you absolutely have to, I would suggest you use an app like Freeform that comes free with ios or sign up to Miro, where you can add sticky notes, draw, type, or handwrite comments.

3. Track

Tracking helps you achieve and maintain goals. In the same way that stepping on a scale every morning can help you maintain a healthy weight, tracking spending or saving can help you achieve your goal.

I have a friend who pinned the energy consumption of the shared house she was living in on her fridge. After six months, the energy bills had decreased 25%. She didn't do anything other than track and place this tracking in a visible place.

So, feel free to ditch the traditional spreadsheets and opt for a colorful and engaging approach. Create a "Goal-o-Meter" poster where you can visually track your progress, and make sure to put it somewhere highly visible. Use different colors and stickers to mark each milestone achieved. Seeing your progress visually can be incredibly motivating and give you a sense of accomplishment.

Remember, financial goals are like stepping stones to your dreams. Like other goals, break them down into bite-sized pieces to make them more manageable. Set smaller, achievable targets that contribute to your overall goal. Celebrate each milestone reached with a mini dance party and a high-five to yourself or your budget buddy. Embrace the joy of progress, no matter how small.

4. BUDGETING WITH ADHD

Budgeting can sound as exciting as going to the dentist. But keep the creativity going once you have your long-term goal and know what you're doing it for. It doesn't have to be complicated, and it doesn't have to be perfect. It can be just as quirky as you as long as it works. So keep your sticky notes and felt tips out, and let me break down the steps to create a simple budget in no time:

1. Set goals

So you should have that part nailed by now through your gorgeous vision board. But it can be helpful to summarize it in one word or one image. Are you saving for a holiday, an emergency fund, or paying debt?

2. Audit

Check your monthly income and your monthly expenses. Write them down into two columns. Thanks to paying everything by card these days, it should be fairly easy to do just by looking at your bank statement.

3. Categorize

You might have an app already doing that for you, but this is the time for your highlighters to shine. Create a few broad categories like rent, groceries, entertainment, etc. Go through your expenses and categorize away, my friend.

4. Group

Determine which category is a fixed expense and which is variable. For instance, your rent is fixed; it's the same every month. But your entertainment, how much you spend on going out, is different every month. This will help you prioritize later.

5. Budget

This is the moment you've been waiting for! Now that you have the facts, you can plan. Check how much is left from your income after expenses and reallocate the funds to achieve your goal.

6. Use the power of technology

I highly recommend you start by doing this on paper first, especially if it is your first-ever budget. But once you've got a clear idea, you might want to move digitally for the budgeting stage. It will cut the mental math and help you with the next steps. Have a look at apps like Mint, or You Need A Budget (YNAB).

7. Review

Put time aside in your diary each month to review and make the necessary adjustments based on the last month.

I know it might sound daunting, so I've included a budget planner in the Empowered ADHD Planners Pack. It will help you visualize those different categories, and you can just fill it out.

It doesn't have to be a lengthy and complicated process. If it helps, you could even take yourself somewhere nice to do it and treat yourself to a fancy coffee (if your budget allows, of course). Just print the budget planner, bring some fancy pens, or do it on your tablet if you're all fancy digital. Can't remember where you stored that pdf? That's okay, you can go and download the planners again here: bit.ly/EmpoweredPlanners

Budgeting will help you with spending and saving, of course, but it will also help you feel more in control and might help reduce any anxiety you might have around money. Now, there are times when things can go terribly wrong, and we head into the debt danger zone. So let's address that too.

5. Manage and Avoid Debt

Let's get serious for a second. Debt can be grueling, and ADHD can make it so that we are more predisposed to it. So let's talk about a few ways in which we can both avoid and manage debt. By the way, this is just my two cents and ideas to get you started, but it is not legal or financial advice.

Track Your Expenses

Basically, all the techniques we just went through a minute ago. By tracking your expenses, you gain clarity on where your money is going and can identify areas where you can make adjustments. The best way to avoid debt is to never start, so by tracking your expenses, you learn to live within your means.

Prioritize Debt Repayment

If you have existing debts, such as credit card balances or loans, prioritize paying them off. Consider using the debt snowball or debt avalanche method. With the snowball method, you focus on paying off the smallest debt first while making minimum payments on the others. The avalanche method, on the other hand, involves tackling the debt with the highest interest rate first. Choose the approach that best suits your situation and commit to regular payments.

Automate Savings

Make saving effortless by automating the process. Set up automatic transfers from your checking account to a dedicated savings account. This technique ensures that a portion of your income goes directly into savings without you having to think about it. Over time, your savings will grow steadily, contributing to your financial security.

Build an Emergency Fund

Establishing an emergency fund is crucial for financial stability. Aim to save three to six months' worth of living expenses to prepare for unexpected events, such as job loss or medical emergencies. Set aside a portion of your income specifically for your emergency fund until you reach your desired target.

Seek Professional Advice

If your debt is debilitating, or you find managing debts and saving challenging, don't hesitate to seek guidance from a financial advisor or credit counselor. You might be able to find free advice depending on where you live.

Keep in mind that learning the know-how of all things money isn't a one-sitting type of task. You're going to have to be patient with yourself. But with the techniques provided in this chapter, your journey should definitely become easier. If you mess up along the way, don't sweat it. You'll get a hang of it soon enough! You don't have to be perfect, remember?

CHAPTER NINE

empowered social and romantic life

HOW TO NAVIGATE THE FRIEND-ZONE, THE LOVE-ZONE, AND EVERYTHING IN BETWEEN

LET'S GET REAL: ADHD can have a big impact on our social lives. It's no secret that our ADHD symptoms can sometimes make things a little, well, interesting. Our minds wander, our impulsivity kicks in, and we might see rejection in all the wrong places. But we're also obviously amazing, and we have the power to shape our social and romantic life with a little self-awareness and the right tools.

We will dive into various techniques and strategies to empower you to build fulfilling relationships, create meaningful connections, and embrace the beautiful chaos that comes with ADHD. And yes, even a sprinkle of romance advice [cue the butterflies].

1. ADHD AND SOCIAL LIFE

So, picture this: you're engaged in a riveting conversation, and suddenly, ADHD decides to take the wheel and steer us into the land of daydreams. Oops! Sorry, folks, I was just busy solving the world's mysteries inside my head.

That's just an example. We could also mention the interrupting and the getting lost in our own long-winded stories. And then, there is punctuality. Time seems to play hide-and-seek with us, disappearing faster than we can say, "I'll be there in a jiffy." And oh, the memory lapses! Birthdays, previous conversations, thank you notes – they can slip through our minds like a stealthy ninja. It's not that we don't care; it's just that our thoughts have a way of doing their own acrobatics.

So you got the idea: we're not short of symptoms that can impact our social life. But let's dive deeper into a few that might be a bit more intrusive than the others.

WINNING THE INTERRUPTION GAME

We have this incredible enthusiasm bubbling inside us that just can't wait to burst out into the conversation. We're like popcorn kernels ready to pop at any moment!

Now, why do we do it? Well, it's not because we don't care about what others have to say. Quite the opposite, actually! We fear that if we don't blurt out our brilliant thoughts right away, they might slip through the cracks of our busy minds. It's the keenness to share our ideas and the worry that we'll forget them that often lead us down the path of interrupting. I know that, you know that, but maybe the people around us don't know that.

So, go tell them now. Yes, it's okay to put the book down. Let's start by acknowledging our tendency to interrupt. Share the fun fact with your friends, family, or colleagues that your enthusiasm sometimes gets the better of you. Trust me, they'll appreciate your honesty and might even find it endearing!

Now, you've seen earlier that while at work you can jot your thoughts down for later, but it might not be ideal at a dinner party. So when you catch yourself interrupting, it's time to put on your graceful recovery moves. After interrupting someone, quickly follow it up with a sincere "Sorry, what were you saying?" or a thoughtful follow-up question to show that you value their input. It's like giving them a VIP ticket to jump back into the conversation.

SURFING THE OVERSHARING AVALANCHE

Let's talk about over-sharing, shall we? As ADHD champions of candid conversations, we have a knack for opening up the floodgates of information without a moment's hesitation. It's like our mouths are equipped with turbo boosters, ready to spill out all the juicy details!

You see, my fellow over-sharers, it's not that we don't appreciate the concept of boundaries. It's just that we have this insatiable desire to connect with others on a deeper level. We wear our hearts on our sleeves and our thoughts on our tongues, making it hard to hold back those fascinating tidbits of our lives. Just like enthusiastic interrupting, those who love you will probably find it endearing if you recognize this tendency.

But there are ways to navigate the treacherous waters of over-sharing with finesse and a splash of self-awareness for other situations.

First, let's gauge the situation before unleashing our personal anecdotes and intimate stories. Is it an appropriate setting for sharing the nitty-gritty details of your life? If not, take a moment to rein in your enthusiasm and save those gems for a more suitable time.

Then, take a deep breath and consider the needs and comfort levels of those around you. Not everyone may be ready to dive into the depths of your experiences, so it's important to respect their boundaries. Remember, it's all about finding that delicate balance between vulnerability and discretion.

DEALING WITH RSD AND SOCIAL ISOLATION

Remember Rejection Sensitive Dysphoria? That moment when a simple comment or a perceived rejection can send our emotions on a bumpy ride to the moon? It's like having a hyperactive emotional radar.

Imagine you're at a social gathering, feeling all excited and ready to mingle. But suddenly, someone shoots a glance your way, and your mind goes into overdrive, decoding every microexpression as a sign of rejection. You start spiraling into thoughts like, "Oh no, they must hate me! I must have said something wrong! I'm a social disaster!" And just like that, you find yourself feeling isolated, even in a room full of people.

It's important to remember, though, that we have the power to rise above it. How, you ask? By being kind to ourselves and recognizing that our perceptions aren't always reality. Instead of jumping to conclusions and assuming the worst, let's challenge those negative thoughts with a splash of positivity. Remember those affirmations from Chapter 4? Well, you've practiced them, so they are second nature once you're at that party, right?

The next time you catch yourself feeling isolated because of RSD, take a moment to pause and reframe those self-defeating thoughts. Remind yourself that you're unique, lovable, and worthy of connection. Embrace the fact that we all have our own quirks, and it's what makes us beautifully human.

2. Make it last forever...

...*Friendship never ends*. Not a Spice Girls fan? Okay, but still, friendship is the magical ingredient that adds flavor to our lives!

But not so fast, my fellow social butterflies; let's address the burning desire to fill our diaries with endless events. Oh, the excitement of non-stop socializing and back-to-back events! But hold your horses, because pacing is key. We've learned the hard way that overloading our schedules can lead to spectacular burnout. So remember to sprinkle some much-needed downtime in between those social gatherings. It's all about finding that sweet spot between connection and self-care.

Finding Your People

Now, let's talk about finding your tribe, your squad, your neurodivergent crew! In this vast digital world, there are countless online and in-real-life communities just waiting to welcome you with open arms. Whether it's a local gathering or a virtual hangout on social media, you'll discover a vibrant network of kindred spirits who understand and support you. So join a few groups, dip your toes in different communities, and choose the one that resonates with your beautiful, unique self.

Remember, friendships are like gardens that need nurturing. Communication is the magic fertilizer that helps them bloom:

healthy boundaries and open conversations are the secret sauce to flourishing friendships. Sounds tricky? Keep reading.

QUALITY OVER QUANTITY

In the realm of friendship, focus on quality over quantity. Your value is not measured by the number of "friends" you've got. Instead, let's curate a tight-knit circle of sympathetic souls who lift us up and make us feel like the superheroes we truly are.

Bid farewell to toxic relationships that drain our energy faster than a malfunctioning power outlet. Surround yourself with people who inspire and support you on your quest for greatness. And dare I say, people who love you just as you are, interrupting, daydreaming, oversharing, and all.

You see, my friends - we're friends by now, no? - here's the thing: boundaries are like our trusty superhero capes, protecting us from things that don't align with our desires, needs, or values. I know it can be hard for both us and the person on the other end, but it's time to put on those capes! Learning to ask for what we need and speaking up for what we struggle with is a superpower we can and should all cultivate.

So imagine this: you're out with friends and they suggest going to a loud, crowded bar. But wait, your ADHD brain knows that sensory overload is not your cup of tea. So what do you do? You muster up the courage to say, "Hey, I'd love to hang out with you, but I'd prefer a quieter environment. How about grabbing a drink in that new place that has no background music?" Boom! You've just set a boundary like a boss!

See what we did there? We used a three steps boundaries setting formula:

1. **The no**: Clearly state what doesn't work for you. A.k.a stand up for your needs, because people can't guess what they are.
2. **The yes**: Make it clear you appreciate the offer and that it is not a rejection of them (unless it is, then just politely decline). They have feelings, too.
3. **The counter-offer**: Offer an alternative. And that is only if you genuinely want to nurture that relationship. If you don't, there is no obligation, just skip this step.

We're not superheroes, but we do have the power to shape our social interactions and create a space where we feel comfortable and respected. It might take a bit of practice, but setting boundaries is a skill worth cultivating as it is the cornerstone of many relationships.

Oh boy, I think I should write a whole book about this. Us folks with ADHD seem to fall pretty easily into the treacherous territory of people-pleasing!

So let's discuss the importance of saying "no." We've all been there, trying to be everything to everyone, juggling tasks like a circus performer. But fear not, my friends, for we have the power to break free from this exhausting cycle.

We've already learned the three steps formula to setting boundaries; now let's look at the 5 steps to saying *no, nada, niet, nein, lo, la, non!*

1. **Delay the answer**: Always start by saying, "Let me get back to you." We often say "yes" because we feel pressured to give an answer.
2. **Ponder**: Take the time to think about what you want. Is it "not in a million years," or is it just not the right time, the right setting, etc? If it's the latter, you can use the boundary-setting formula and offer an alternative. If it's "never," move on to the next step.
3. **Decline politely**: Say something like "I'm so sorry, I won't be able to help you with this," or "I'm afraid I can't make it."
4. **No explanation needed**: Don't offer an explanation. You don't have to justify yourself.
5. **Help**: But only by offering an alternative solution that doesn't mean *you* are doing it later. It means helping them find another solution, like "Have you asked Will?" or "Would it be possible to take a taxi? Would you like a number?"

Learning to say "no" is another superhero muscle that needs flexing. So, let's practice the fine art of politely declining and reclaiming our precious time and energy.

Just remember that setting boundaries is simply a way to gently communicate our needs, express our limits, and kindly assert ourselves when necessary. Friendships should be a harmonious dance, not a never-ending tug-of-war.

3. Love in the Time of ADHD

First, let's dive into the science behind falling in love. According to love experts (a.k.a. scientists), attraction creates a magical concoction of dopamine and serotonin in our brains. It's like a chemical love potion that makes our hearts flutter, and our minds go, "Wow, this person is amazing!" No wonder we're drawn to the exhilarating rush of romance!

So with those hits of dopamine, love in the time of ADHD can become a rollercoaster ride of emotions, distractions, and endless possibilities, hopping from one symptom ride to another. All the usual suspects are here: impulsivity, daydreaming, emotional dysregulation, RSD, and many more. So let's embark on this wild journey together and address the quirks and challenges that come with it. Buckle up, lovebirds!

5 Habits to Build a Strong Relationship

Building a strong relationship with ADHD in the mix is like a dance party where coordination might not always be our strong suit, but boy, do we bring the energy! Let's explore some essential steps to groove our way to a healthy and thriving partnership.

1. Take responsibility

First things first, let's take responsibility. It's important for both partners to acknowledge and understand how ADHD can impact the relationship. Embrace a sense of ownership and work together as a team to navigate the ups and downs.

It's about knowing yourselves and how you work. ADHD is not a free pass for being a nightmare; equally, it doesn't make you stupid or lazy, so you shouldn't be infantilized. Remember, it takes two to tango, and mutual support and understanding go a long way.

2. Communication

Communication is the DJ that keeps the relationship beat flowing smoothly. Open and honest dialogue is the key. Use the formulas for healthy boundaries and say "no" with your partner as well. It might look simply like this: "Sorry, I can't listen to your work story right now, I am interested, but I'm sorting out a play date, so if you give me two minutes, I'll be able to listen properly."

We've already covered handling difficult conversations at work, so when it comes to it, you can refer back to those handy tips and tricks which can apply at home, too.

Effective communication means active listening, expressing needs and concerns, and finding compromises that work for both of you.

3. Planning the future

Discuss your dreams, aspirations, and goals as a couple. This helps foster a sense of unity and direction, ensuring that you're both on the same page when it comes to building a life together. It's like choreographing a synchronized routine that keeps you moving in harmony. And, yes, it can imply the financial goals we've been talking about.

4. Celebraaaaaate good times, come on (again)

Don't forget to hit the dance floor and celebrate your strengths and accomplishments! I mean metaphorically, but you're welcome to take it literally.

ADHD may present its challenges, but it also brings a unique set of strengths and talents. State what works and what you're both doing well. Take the time to appreciate and acknowledge each other's positive qualities.

5. Spending time together

Prioritize quality time together, a time when you switch off from distractions (yes, the phone, too) and you're fully present. In the whirlwind of life, it's crucial to carve out dedicated moments for connection and shared experiences. Whether it's a romantic date night, a weekend getaway, or simply cuddling on the couch, these moments nurture the bond between you. Think of it as stepping into a spotlight: give your relationship and your partner the attention they deserve and leave everything else in the dark for a few hours.

4. SEX, INTIMACY, AND ADHD

"Let's talk about sex, baby, Let's talk about you and me, Let's talk about all the good things, And the bad things that may be..." Okay, not a Salt-n-Pepa fan? That's cool. Let's explore the challenges, the myths, and of course, the strategies around sex when ADHD gets in the way!

Sometimes our minds can drift away faster than a feather on the breeze, making it challenging to maintain focus and connection during those intimate moments.

Comorbidities, like anxiety and depression, can also throw a little extra spice into the mix. It's like having a few additional backup dancers on stage, making things more complex.

ADHD can also impact sexual function and satisfaction, leading to difficulties with arousal, desire, and orgasm. And sometimes, the biggest challenges are not sexual but emotional and revolve around guilt and shame.

A 2023 research published in the *International Journal of Environmental Research and Public Health* distributed a survey to 1392 people, found that people with ADHD "were more adventurous in sexual interests and practices and substantially less satisfied with their partners, both sexually and generally."

But hey, let's not let that discourage us! Understanding these challenges can help us find creative solutions.

Impulsive sexual behavior and risk-taking are often associated with ADHD, and that same study confirms it: "Females had younger onset of sexual activities, used contraception less frequently, had more sexual partners and practiced more infidelity." But just because we have ADHD doesn't mean we're constantly swinging from chandeliers like love-struck acrobats. Actually, many women with ADHD report being hyposexual, which means they don't have much interest in sexual activity.

What's certain is that, once again, there is not enough scientific research on the subject. And once again... Can you guess?... Bingo! The research out there mostly focuses on men.

So, how do we navigate these choppy seas?

7 Strategies to Get Your Marvin Gaye on

Or something like that. Anyway, here are seven tips that can help.

1. Self-love

No, not that kind, though, of course, there is nothing wrong with that. I'm talking about coping with shame, guilt, and self-doubt related to ADHD and sexuality.

Remember, ADHD is just a part of who you are and doesn't define your worth or capabilities in the bedroom. Be kind to yourself and use the tools in Chapter 4 to challenge any negative thoughts or self-judgment that may arise. Embrace self-acceptance and focus on the unique strengths you bring to the relationship.

2. Communication (again)

Openly discussing our desires, needs, and concerns with our partner helps build trust, understanding, and intimacy. Make sure you're also discussing any challenges you may face, such as difficulties with arousal, focus, or impulsivity. By sharing your experiences, you can work together to find solutions and make adjustments that meet both of your needs. It will also help dissipate misunderstandings related to sexual functioning.

3. Create time and space

ADHD thrives on structure, and incorporating routines into your sexual activities can be beneficial. Set aside dedicated time for intimacy, create a comfortable environment, and minimize sensory distractions as much as possible. Establishing a predictable environment can enhance focus, reduce impulsivity, and develop a sense of safety and consistency.

4. Mindfulness and relaxation (yes, again)

Anxiety and stress can impact sexual functioning. Engage in mindfulness exercises, such as deep breathing or meditation, to calm your mind and reduce racing thoughts. Prioritize self-care, engage in activities that help you relax, and manage stress to create a conducive environment for intimacy.

Besides, remember what we said about mindfulness? It's not just about relaxing and meditation; it's about bringing your focus to the moment. So you can totally apply it here! Focus on that touch, that look, that sound. Yeah, you got the idea.

5. Pleasure

Now, let's address the elephant in the bedroom – pleasure! ADHD might throw a few curveballs our way, but it doesn't mean we can't have a fulfilling and enjoyable sex life. Exploring different techniques, experimenting with new sensations, and embracing a sense of adventure can add some extra sizzle to the bedroom.

6. Intimacy and connection

Intimacy isn't just about the physical aspect. It also encompasses emotional closeness and deep connection. Encourage non-sexual forms of intimacy, such as touch, cuddling, and affectionate gestures. Engage in meaningful conversations, share your dreams and desires, and actively listen to your partner's thoughts and feelings.

7. Quality time

Remember how quality time can help build a strong relationship? Well, it can help here too. Disconnect from distractions like screens and truly focus on connecting with your partner.

If ADHD symptoms significantly impact your sexual relationship or if comorbid conditions like anxiety or depression are present, consider seeking professional help. A therapist experienced in working with ADHD and sexual health should be able to provide guidance, support, and specific strategies tailored to your unique situation.

Remember, building intimacy and connection takes time and effort, but the journey can be fun and rewarding. Embrace your uniqueness, be open to learning and growing together, and enjoy the journey of deepening your emotional bond with your partner. You've got this!

conclusion

And so, my ADHD sisters, we've reached the end of this whirlpool of an adventure through the world of ADHD. We've explored the tangles of tidying, the perils of people-pleasing, how to find harmony with hormones, the magic of mindfulness, the comfort of CBT, and even the spectacular particulars of sensory processing. It's been quite the journey, hasn't it?

But you've come out of it armed with a boatload of knowledge and a lighthearted look at our everyday struggles. You're now kitted with all the tools you need to navigate ADHD's windy shores. All you need to do is set sail with a newfound sense of confidence that you've got everything you need for that journey. Sure, there will be big waves, maybe even storms. Who knows? Life happens. You might even get lost a little.

But now that those tools are yours, trust that you can always open the toolbox and pick the perfect one for you. Remember, managing ADHD is a dance: sometimes graceful and sometimes downright chaotic, but always uniquely yours.

So as you step into the wild and wonderful world ahead, may your dopamine levels soar, your executive functions remain sharp, and your ADHD-fueled creativity light up the sky. May you find peace amid the clutter, joy in the kitchen chaos, and triumph in your own special way of doing things.

Always remember that you are not alone on this ADHD roller-coaster. Embrace your quirks, celebrate your strengths, and always keep a sense of humor close at hand. May your days be filled with focus, your sleep restful, your dreams reach new heights, and your journey be as colorful and vibrant as your brilliant, ADHD-infused mind.

Keep rocking and rolling, and always embrace the quirks that make you so uniquely you. Life may throw you a curveball or two, but with determination and a sprinkle of mindfulness, you'll conquer any challenge that comes your way.

But wait! Before you go off on your new ADHD adventures, I have another request for you. If this book has helped you untangle the knots, find clarity amidst the chaos, and equipped you with the tools to navigate the twists and turns of ADHD, I invite you to share your experience by leaving a review on Amazon. Your words have the power to inspire others who are seeking solace and support on their own ADHD journeys.

Leaving a review is as easy as the flick of a wrist. Just head over to the book's page on Amazon, scroll down to the "Customer Reviews" section, and click on the "Write a customer review" button. Then pour your heart out as you would talk to a friend, share your insights and your favorite parts, and let the world know how this book has made a difference in your life.

By leaving an honest review, you become a guiding light, helping fellow ADHD-ers find the support and resources they need. Your words can be the beacon that leads them toward clarity and confidence. Together, let's create a community of empowerment and understanding where every woman with ADHD can find the tools and guidance they deserve.

With boundless energy and infinite gratitude,

Estelle Rose

how to leave a review

So are you ready to share the Empowered ADHD love and support other women to thrive on their own ADHD journeys?

Leaving a review on Amazon is as easy as 1-2-3:

1. Visit the book's page on Amazon.
2. Scroll down to the "Customer Reviews" section.
3. Click on the "Write a customer review" button.

Once you're there, pour your heart out as if you were talking to a friend. Here are some ideas to get you started:

- Share your insights and favorite parts of the book.
- Describe how the book has made a difference in your life.
- Describe the tone of the book and what makes it special.

Feel free to get creative! Sometimes images speak louder than words, so add a photo or a video to complement your review and make it more personal.

To leave a review, please visit: mybook.to/empoweredADHDbook

 **You can also scan the QR code** below to go directly to the review page.

Spark that warm and fuzzy feeling of empowering others and unlocking a collective strength that uplifts everyone involved.

Your authentic review holds the remarkable power to ignite a spark within others, guiding them towards the support and resources they yearn for.

Your contribution is instrumental in creating this transformative journey of empowerment. Thank you so much for being an essential part of it.

IT'S NOT TOO LATE

Get your
Empowered ADHD Planners Pack,
the perfect companion to this book,
to start taking control of your time,
racing thoughts and emotions
immediately.

A GIFT
FOR
YOU

Free planners

Download now

DOWNLOAD NOW

Follow this link:
bit.ly /
EmpoweredPlanners

or scan the
QR code

also by estelle rose

BRAIN-BOOSTING FOOD FOR WOMEN WITH ADHD

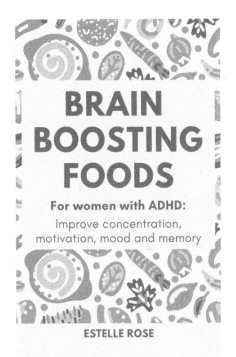

about the author

Estelle Rose, author of *Empowered Women with ADHD* and *Brain-Boosting Food for Women with ADHD,* is dedicated to helping women with ADHD thrive.

Her guides provide practical strategies for managing symptoms and achieving goals. With a late diagnosis, Estelle understands the unique challenges of ADHD.

She explored psychology, therapies, neuroscience, self-hypnosis, meditation, nutrition, and coaching, gaining valuable insights to manage her own ADHD. This transformative experience fueled her desire to share her experiences and expertise with others.

Estelle's writing is compassionate, insightful, and informative, offering practical tips and strategies. Her warm and engaging style provides invaluable resources for women at all stages of their ADHD journey.

Estelle's commitment to empowering women with ADHD shines through, helping women with ADHD thrive and embrace their unique strengths, and making her books essential for those newly diagnosed or who have been living with the condition for years.

references

ADDitude Editors. (2023, June 5). *PMS and ADHD: How the Menstrual Cycle Intensifies Symptoms.* ADDitude. https://www.additudemag.com/pms-adhd-hormones-menstrual-cycle/

Antiglio, D. (2018). *The Life-Changing Power of Sophrology: A practical guide to reducing stress and living up to your full potential.* Hachette UK.

Beheshti, A., Chavanon, M., & Christiansen, H. (2020). Emotion dysregulation in adults with attention deficit hyperactivity disorder: a meta-analysis. BMC Psychiatry, 20(1). https://doi.org/10.1186/s12888-020-2442-7

Christiansen, L. (2020). *Effects of Exercise on Cognitive Performance in Children and Adolescents with ADHD: Potential Mechanisms and Evidence-based Recommendations.* Drcmr. https://www.academia.edu/42427312/Effects_of_Exercise_on_Cognitive_Performance_in_Children_and_Adolescents_with_ADHD_Potential_Mechanisms_and_Evidence_based_Recommendations

Clear, J. (2018). *Atomic Habits: An Easy & Proven Way to Build Good Habits & Break Bad Ones.* National Geographic Books.

Comorbidity of attention deficit hyperactivity disorder with conduct, depressive, anxiety, and other disorders. (1991). American Journal of Psychiatry, 148(5), 564–577. https://doi.org/10.1176/ajp.148.5.564

Creswell, J. D., Dutcher, J. M., P. Klein, W. M., Harris, P. R., & Levine, J. M. (2013). *Self-Affirmation Improves Problem-Solving under Stress.* PLOS ONE, 8 (5), e62593. https://doi.org/10.1371/journal.pone.0062593

Dol, K. S. (2019). *Effects of a yoga nidra on the life stress and self-esteem in university students.* Complementary Therapies in Clinical Practice, 35, 232–236. https://doi.org/10.1016/j.ctcp.2019.03.004

Dorani, Brown, Bijlenga, F., Thomas, Sarah. (2018). *Premenstrual Symptoms in Women with ADHD: A Comparison with Women Without ADHD.* Journal of Clinical Psychology, 74(12), 1283–1293. https://doi.org/10.1002/jclp.22561

Ferreira-Vorkapic, C., Borba-Pinheiro, C. J., Marchioro, M., & Santana, D. O. (2018). *The impact of yoga Nidra and seated meditation on the mental health of college professors.* International Journal of Yoga, 11(3), 215. https://doi.org/10.4103/ijoy.ijoy_57_17

Galantino, M. L., Tiger, R., Brooks, J. D., Jang, S., & Wilson, K. (2019). *Impact of Somatic Yoga and Meditation on Fall Risk, Function, and Quality of Life for Chemotherapy-Induced Peripheral Neuropathy Syndrome in Cancer Survivors.* Integrative Cancer Therapies, 18, 153473541985062. https://doi.org/10.1177/1534735419850627

Gaume, J., Heather, N., Tober, G., & McCambridge, J. (2018). *A mediation analysis of treatment processes in the UK Alcohol Treatment Trial.* Journal of Consulting and Clinical Psychology, 86(4), 321–329. https://doi.org/10.1037/ccp0000287

Goering, S. (2015).
Rethinking disability: the social model of disability and chronic disease. Current Reviews

in Musculoskeletal Medicine, 8(2), 134–138. https://doi.org/10.1007/s12178-015-9273-z

Green, R. (2022). *ADHD Symptom Spotlight: Emotional Dysregulation.* Verywell Mind. https://www.verywellmind.com/adhd-symptom-spotlight-emotional-dysregulation-5219946

Hinshaw, S. P., Nguyen, P., O'Grady, S. M., & Rosenthal, E. (2021). Annual Research Review: Attention-deficit/hyperactivity disorder in girls and women: underrepresentation, longitudinal processes, and key directions. *Journal of Child Psychology and Psychiatry,* 63(4), 484–496. https://doi.org/10.1111/jcpp.13480

Humphreys, K. L., McGoron, L., Sheridan, M. A., McLaughlin, K. A., Fox, N. A., Nelson, C. A., & Zeanah, C. H. (2015). *High-Quality Foster Care Mitigates Callous-Unemotional Traits Following Early Deprivation in Boys: A Randomized Controlled Trial.* Journal of the American Academy of Child and Adolescent Psychiatry, 54(12), 977–983. https://doi.org/10.1016/j.jaac.2015.09.010

Hwang, W. J., Lee, T. Y., Kim, N. S., & Kwon, J. S. (2021). The Role of Estrogen Receptors and Their Signaling across Psychiatric Disorders. *International Journal of Molecular Sciences,* 22(1), 373. https://doi.org/10.3390/ijms22010373

Kelly, K., & Ramundo, P. (2006). *You Mean I'm Not Lazy, Stupid or Crazy?!: The Classic Self-Help Book for Adults with Attention Deficit Disorder.* Simon and Schuster.

Ko, E. M., Lim, W. E., & Griffiths, M. D. (2020). *The Impact of Social Media on Individuals with ADHD: A Systematic Review and Meta-Analysis.* Cyberpsychology, Behavior, and Social Networking, 23(1), 1–10. https://doi.org/10.1089/cyber.2019.29021

Kuo, F. Y., & Taylor, A. B. (2004). *A Potential Natural Treatment for Attention-Deficit/Hyperactivity Disorder: Evidence From a National Study.* American Journal of Public Health, 94(9), 1580–1586. https://doi.org/10.2105/ajph.94.9.1580

Linehan, M. M., Dimeff, L. A., Reynolds, S. A., Comtois, K. A., Welch, S. S., Heagerty, P. J., & Kivlahan, D. R. (2002). *Dialectical behavior therapy versus comprehensive validation therapy plus 12-step for the treatment of opioid dependent women meeting criteria for borderline personality disorder.* Drug and Alcohol Dependence, 67(1), 13–26. https://doi.org/10.1016/s0376-8716(02)00011-x

Linehan, M. M., Schmidt, H. J., Dimeff, L. A., Craft, J. C., Kanter, J. W., & Comtois, K. A. (1999). *Dialectical Behavior Therapy for Patients with Borderline Personality Disorder and Drug-Dependence.* American Journal on Addictions, 8(4), 279–292. https://doi.org/10.1080/105504999305686

Managing Money and ADHD: Money Management Schedule - CHADD. (2019, February 26). CHADD. https://chadd.org/for-adults/managing-money-and-adhd-money-management-schedule/

Mitchell, J. C., Zylowska, L., & Kollins, S. H. (2015). *Mindfulness Meditation Training for Attention-Deficit/Hyperactivity Disorder in Adulthood: Current Empirical Support, Treatment Overview, and Future Directions.* Cognitive and Behavioral Practice, 22(2), 172–191. https://doi.org/10.1016/j.cbpra.2014.10.002

Pacheco, D., & Pacheco, D. (2023). *ADHD and Sleep.* Sleep Foundation. https://www.sleepfoundation.org/mental-health/adhd-and-sleep

Pcc, L. R. (2021, September 17). *How to Declutter with an ADHD Brain: Organization Solutions for Real Life.* ADDitude. https://www.additudemag.com/slideshows/how-to-declutter-adhd/

Pew Research Center. (2023, May 17). *Many US Twitter users have taken a break from Twitter, and some may not use it a year from now.* Pew Research Center.

https://www.pewresearch.org/short-reads/2023/05/17/majority-of-us-twitter-users-say-theyve-taken-a-break-from-the-platform-in-the-past-year/

Reid, R. L., Hakendorf, P., & Prosser, B. (2002). *Use of Psychostimulant Medication for ADHD in South Australia.* Journal of the American Academy of Child and Adolescent Psychiatry, 41(8), 906–913. https://doi.org/10.1097/00004583-200208000-00008

Rose, E. (2023). *Brain-Boosting Foods for Women with ADHD: Improve Concentration, Motivation, Mood, and Memory.* Rosali Publishing.

Schnitzler, A., & Gross, J. (2005). *Normal and pathological oscillatory communication in the brain.* Nature Reviews Neuroscience, 6(4), 285–296. https://doi.org/10.1038/nrn1650

Stevens, L. M., Kuczek, T., Burgess, J., Hurt, E., & Arnold, L. E. (2011). *Dietary Sensitivities and ADHD Symptoms: Thirty-five Years of Research.* Clinical Pediatrics, 50(4), 279–293. https://doi.org/10.1177/0009922810384728

Strang, J.F., Kenworthy, L., Dominska, A. et al. Increased Gender Variance in Autism Spectrum Disorders and Attention Deficit Hyperactivity Disorder. *Arch Sex Behav* 43, 1525–1533 (2014). https://doi.org/10.1007/s10508-014-0285-3

Thapar, A., & Cooper, M. (2016). *Attention deficit hyperactivity disorder.* The Lancet, 387(10024), 1240–1250. https://doi.org/10.1016/s0140-6736(15)00238-x

Thapar, A., Cooper, M., Eyre, O., & Langley, K. (2013). *Practitioner Review: What have we learnt about the causes of ADHD?* Journal of Child Psychology and Psychiatry, 54(1), 3–16. https://doi.org/10.1111/j.1469-7610.2012.02611.x

Thrower, E., Cheung, A. S., Pang, K. C., & Zajac, J. D. (2020). *Prevalence of Autism Spectrum Disorder and Attention-Deficit Hyperactivity Disorder Amongst Individuals with Gender Dysphoria: A Systematic Review.* Journal of Autism and Developmental Disorders, 50(3), 695–706. https://doi.org/10.1007/s10803-019-04298-1

Vysniauske, R., Verburgh, L., Oosterlaan, J., & Molendijk, M. L. (2020). *The Effects of Physical Exercise on Functional Outcomes in the Treatment of ADHD: A Meta-Analysis.* Journal of Attention Disorders, 24(5), 644–654. https://doi.org/10.1177/1087054715627489

Wolcott M. D. (2022). *Damaged, discouraged and defeated? How mindset may offer hope for healing.* Medical education, 56(5), 477–479. https://doi.org/10.1111/medu.14740

Yildirim, B. I., Fiş, N. P., Akgül, G. Y., & Ayaz, A. S. (2017). *Gender dysphoria and attention problems: possible clue for biological underpinnings.* Psychiatry and Clinical Psychopharmacology, 27(3), 283–290. https://doi.org/10.1080/24750573.2017.1354417

Young, S., Klassen, L. J., Reitmeier, S. D., Matheson, J. D., & Gudjonsson, G. H. (2023). Let's Talk about Sex… and ADHD: Findings from an Anonymous Online Survey. *International Journal of Environmental Research and Public Health, 20(3).* https://doi.org/10.3390/ijerph20032037

Zylowska, L., Ackerman, D. L., Yang, M. C., Futrell, J. L., Horton, N. L., Hale, T. S., Pataki, C., & Smalley, S. L. (2008). *Mindfulness Meditation Training in Adults and Adolescents With ADHD.* Journal of Attention Disorders, 11(6), 737–746. https://doi.org/10.1177/1087054707308502

Zylowska, L., & Siegel, D. J., MD. (2012). *The Mindfulness Prescription for Adult ADHD: An Eight-step Program for Strengthening Attention, Managing Emotions, and Achieving Your Goals.* Shambhala Publications.

Milton Keynes UK
Ingram Content Group UK Ltd.
UKHW041729220124
436463UK00004B/85